Also by Jennifer Appel

The Buttercup Bake Shop Cookbook
The Magnolia Bakery Cookbook (with Allysa Torey)

Buttercup Bakes at Home

More Than **75** New Recipes

from Manhattan's Premier Bake Shop

for Tempting Homemade Sweets

Jennifer Appel

PHOTOGRAPHS BY ANN STRATTON

SIMON & SCHUSTER
New York   London   Toronto   Sydney

SIMON & SCHUSTER
Rockefeller Center
1230 Avenue of the Americas
New York, NY 10020

Additional credits:
Marlene Rounds, Photographer's Assistant
Michael Pederson, Food Stylist
Tracy Harler, Food Stylist Assistant
Cathy Cook, Prop Stylist
Tammy Schoenfeld, Prop Stylist Assistant

For information about special discounts for bulk purchases, please contact Simon & Schuster Special
Sales at 1-800-456-6798 or business@simonandschuster.com.

DESIGNED BY JAIME PUTORTI

Manufactured in the United States of America
10 8 6 4 2 1 3 5 7 9
Library of Congress Cataloging-in-Publication Data
Jennifer Appel.
Buttercup bakes at home : more than 75 new recipes from Manhattan's premier bake shop for
tempting homemade sweets / Jennifer Appel ; photographs by Ann Stratton.
p. cm.
1. Baking. 2. Desserts. 3. Buttercup Bake Shop. I. Title.
TX765.A573 2006
641.8'15—dc22
2006045202

ISBN-13: 978-0-7432-7122-6
ISBN-10: 0-7432-7122-X

ACKNOWLEDGMENTS

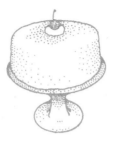

Many thanks again must go to my agent, Carla Glasser, who is always excited by old-fashioned treats, and to my wonderful editor, Sydny Miner, who loves dessert cookbooks as much as my desserts. And, of course, heaps of gratitude go to my wonderful customers, friends, and family who keep inspiring me to create. But most of all, thanks and love to Hernán and Isabel.

Contents

Layer Cakes 31

Cupcakes, Cupcakes, Cupcakes . . . 49

Coffee Cakes, Tube Cakes, and Pound Cakes 63

Buttercup
Bakes at Home

INTRODUCTION

It seems like just yesterday when I first opened the doors to Buttercup Bake Shop one sunny August morning. I remember customers lining up for a taste of our divine creations, and the lines haven't stopped in the six years we have been here. Innumerable cupcakes and countless birthday and special-occasion cakes later, my tiny Midtown bakery is as popular as ever, churning out our from-scratch confections in full view of our devoted customers. Each of our famous cupcakes is lovingly frosted by hand in our front window and our mouthwatering layer cakes are iced and decorated in our glass-enclosed kitchen, as customers watch with their noses pressed against the glass whenever possible.

Seeing customers sit down and enjoy their desserts is a joy. It seems that peeling off the paper to each cupcake transports folks right back to their childhood, and the expressions on their faces are always the same: deep satisfaction and happiness.

Our from-scratch baking is so delicious and down-home that customers try to pass off our desserts as their own! I know this because one day several years ago a woman purchased a birthday cake inscribed for her son's birthday and asked us not to "put the sticker on the box." By sheer coincidence, her son was working nearby and stopped in just for a Buttercup snack. It was quite a funny moment, but all was forgiven, even though the jig was up!

While our popularity has grown over time, so has the list of clientele who enjoy Buttercup's freshly baked goods. More and more folks are hosting parties and events featuring our signature cakes and cupcakes such as Buttercup Golden, Lady Baltimore, and German Chocolate, including the *Today* show, *Live with Regis and Kelly*,

Late Night with Conan O'Brien, *Saturday Night Live*, and Miramax Studios, as well as dozens of television stations, publishing houses, and major magazines. It appears that New Yorkers, famous or otherwise, can't get enough of our sweet creations.

As the desire to bring back the neighborhood bake shop grows, so has my passion to deliver freshly baked all-American desserts to the people who love them. With that in mind, I have plans to bring the neighborhood bake shop to every neighborhood in New York City and even farther, to your favorite city or town. Each bakery will have that same old-fashioned nostalgic charm, with those familiar sights and smells to delight the senses.

While my business has flourished, so has my family. Since my last cookbook was published, I have gotten married to my sweetheart, Hernán. And in case you're wondering, the answer is yes, I made my own wedding cake! It was a simple but beautiful old-fashioned white cake with silky buttercream frosting, adorned with pale ivory buttercream dots and drop flowers.

In 2004, my husband and I welcomed our remarkable daughter into the world, Isabel Eliana. What a treat it will be when she can climb up on a chair in the kitchen and bake with me! I'm sure she'll love to, since she already has a sweet tooth, and with a chef for a father and a baker for a mother, I think a love of food is most certainly in her blood.

As a baker, I'm constantly creating new desserts. This book is a result of that creative desire. While it's hard to pin down my absolute favorites, a few of my new confectionary loves include Drizzled Peanut Butter Chocolate Chunk Cookies, Cranberry Tea Loaf, Black and White Cupcakes, and Butterscotch Pudding. And while rich old-fashioned desserts continue to please our customers, today's crowd also wants a few low-fat, low-sugar treats. So I've whipped up a few recipes to include that satisfy the taste buds but won't necessarily pack on the pounds, like Low-fat Chocolate Bread Pudding with Raspberry Sauce, Teatime Apple Cake, and Splenda-iferous Cream-Filled Vanilla Cupcakes. I've also included a chapter just on cupcakes, as well as one for baking with children. So here are more than seventy-five new recipes that promise to be as enjoyable and easy-to-bake as they are delicious and satisfying to eat.

And if you're in the neighborhood, don't forget to stop in to see us at Buttercup and say hi!

Jennifer

Helpful Hints

Many people claim that cooking is an art, while baking is a science. I like to think of baking as a bit of both, because I find making desserts tremendously satisfying in the creative sense. However, a science it is; basic rules have to be followed in order to produce your desired results. This section is designed to help you avoid the many errors that novice bakers make. By following these simple rules, your results should be worthy of appearing in a bakery each and every day.

I have chosen certain aspects of baking that I think are most important for the reader to know, especially those that relate to my recipes. It's important to know the basics about ovens, pans, equipment, techniques, and ingredients, so that you are armed with the best information before setting out to bake even the most simple desserts.

Creaming Butter

Butter is ideal when used at room temperature, meaning soft enough to hold an impression of your finger when poked. Remove it from the refrigerator about 30 to 45 minutes before you need it. Butter that is too cold will be clumpy, and light and airy cake layers and cupcakes are the result of whipping air into room-temperature butter and sugar; if the creaming process is not done properly, your cakes will be dense and flat as a result.

Ingredients

Before starting any recipe, always read the recipe from beginning to end to make sure that you thoroughly understand it. Then assemble your ingredients and equipment before beginning, to make the process flow more smoothly.

Butter: There is no substitute for butter in baking, and we only use butter in our recipes at the bakery. Using unsalted butter is important because it allows you to control the amount of salt in your recipe.

Chocolate: Use the best-quality chocolate you can find, either domestic or imported. At the bakery, we use only Belgian chocolate. I prefer imported chocolate for all my baking—especially for frostings and ganache, where the flavor is really important. To decorate the tops of cakes with chocolate shavings, you can do so easily using a good vegetable peeler and a room-temperature piece of chocolate.

Cocoa powder: Dutch-process cocoa powder is cocoa powder that has been processed with an alkali to make it darker in color. Feel free to substitute it with regular cocoa powder, which is always unsweetened in this book.

Cream cheese: Like butter, cream cheese should also be taken out of the refrigerator early to soften before using. Do not use whipped cream cheese for baking.

Dry ingredients: Be sure to use the type of flour specified in your recipe; self-rising, cake, and all-purpose flours perform differently, so don't interchange them or you'll wind up with a failed recipe. Flours are best stored at room temperature, tightly sealed. The same goes for granulated and brown sugar. I like to sift cornstarch and confectioners' sugar before using them because they have a tendency to clump. If brown sugar becomes hard, sprinkle it with a few drops of water, wrap it in aluminum foil, and heat it in the oven for 5 minutes to soften. Let it cool before using.

Eggs: I find that large eggs are best for baking and produce the most consistent results. Medium or jumbo eggs can be substituted, but the quantity of eggs will have to be adjusted in the recipe, which may alter your results.

Extracts: Using pure extracts will ensure a better-tasting dessert. I find that imitation extracts impart a weaker flavor.

Fruit: Always choose the freshest, ripest fruit you can find—it makes a big difference in your dessert. This is especially true for bananas, which should always be yellow with brown spots or just on the verge of turning brown.

Milk: Always use whole milk in recipes unless low-fat milk is called for in a particular recipe; I wouldn't substitute anything for whole milk when making layer cakes and cupcakes.

Sugar: My recipes always call for granulated sugar unless stated otherwise.

Measuring

Measuring properly is key in baking—I can't emphasize this enough.

Use the best-quality metal cups and spoons you can find because they are well calibrated for accuracy; cheaper versions are usually slightly off, which will affect your results. Always use glass or Pyrex for measuring liquids, not solid measuring cups.

When measuring dry ingredients, spoon them into a measuring cup and level it off with the edge of a metal spatula. Do the same with measuring spoons. Brown sugar is not usually loosely packed when measured; press and pack it into a cup, and then level it off with a metal spatula. I always specify firmly packed in my recipes; if not, then you may measure it loosely.

When measuring liquid ingredients, place your clear measuring cup on a flat surface to accurately read the amounts. When spooning liquid ingredients, do so over an empty bowl in case of spills. If you measure them over your recipe, you can add too much by accident.

Melting Chocolate

Using a double boiler is the best way to melt chocolate. You want the water in the bottom at just a simmer, but not boiling. Be extra careful when melting white chocolate, however, because it has a lower burning point, so your water should be just barely simmering. You can microwave chocolate too, using a plastic bowl for the chocolate with your microwave on medium power. Stir your chocolate at 30-second intervals to prevent burning, and continue until it is smooth and no pieces remain. Microwave white chocolate for a shorter time between stirrings.

Mixers

At the bakery, we use only 7-quart stand mixers, and mix everything in small batches, which is why our goods have that quality homemade taste. At home, I use a 5-quart version of that mixer. I prefer a stand mixer because it comes with a flat paddle and a wire whip, which is essential for egg whites and meringue recipes. You can use a handheld mixer for almost all of the recipes in this book, but I highly recommend the stand mixer for recipes like angel food cakes and meringue frostings. I also find that a stand mixer is good for standard buttercreams and frostings because it produces a smoother and more supple icing.

I find it handy to have both instruments because you can make one part of a recipe in a stand mixer while whipping the egg whites that go into it with your handheld mixer at the same time.

Oven Thermometers

I frequently hear from customers and readers of my books that they haven't gotten the right results despite following a particular recipe of mine to a T. Knowing the temperature of your oven is key here; use an oven thermometer to make sure your oven is properly calibrated, therefore producing even heat around your product. Uneven heat can cause desserts to burn, bake unevenly, or take longer or shorter to bake than the amount of time recommended in the recipe. Always start with the minimum amount of time stated and check your recipe at that point, or a minute less if you suspect you have a "hot" oven.

Separating and Whipping Egg Whites

It is easier to separate eggs when they are cold. In my opinion, the best instrument to use in separating eggs are your hands. When whipping egg whites, place them in a clean, dry bowl because any addition of fat to the whites will make it difficult to whip them properly. Bring the eggs to room temperature after you separate them, since this is best for optimal baking results.

Sifting

While we use sifters at the bakery, you can also use a kitchen strainer with a very fine mesh. As long as you are aerating the dry goods, it works. I only sift flour for certain recipes, so read the directions carefully. Always sift confectioners' sugar and cornstarch before using because they tend to clump and absorb moisture easily.

Toasting Nuts

I toast all nuts before baking. It takes very little time and creates a noticeable difference when using them in any recipe. In a 350-degree oven, spread the nuts on a baking sheet with high sides. Check on them every 5 minutes or so, leaving them in for no more than 10 to 12 minutes. The nuts will turn a darker color and the oils give off a very fragrant scent, but take care not to let them get too dark or burn. Only toast whole nuts, never chopped or slivered. Chop them after toasting, once the nuts have cooled.

Water Baths for Cheesecakes

Over the years, I've found that the best way to make a great cheesecake is to use a water bath. The water produces steam, which surrounds the cheesecake during the baking process and helps prevent cracks. Use a pan that is at least 2 inches deep, and fill it with about 1 inch of water. Wrap foil around the cheesecake pan to make sure it stays dry. Place your cheesecake in the water bath, and the pan in the oven.

Zesting and Juicing Fruit

While I used to use my old box grater for zesting, the long, slim zester I now have is so useful for baking that it's almost impossible for me to bake without it. Zest only the colorful outer skin of the fruit, leaving the white pith behind, which tends to be bitter. For juicing, I use a two-part hand juicer that catches the pits. There's no substitute for freshly squeezed juice in almost any recipe.

Happy baking!

Cookies and Bars

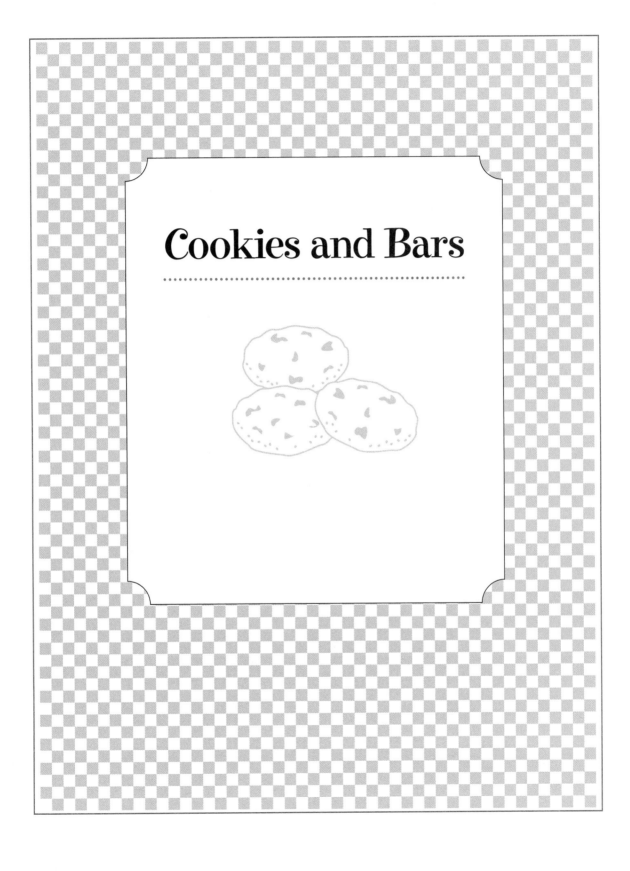

Caramel-Topped Toffee Pecan Blondies

Preheat oven to 350 degrees.

Grease and flour an 8-inch square baking pan.

In a medium bowl, combine the flour, baking powder, and salt. Set aside.

In a large mixing bowl, on the medium speed of an electric mixer, beat the eggs for about 1 to 2 minutes. Next add the sugar and brown sugar and beat until thick and creamy. Add to this the melted butter, vanilla, and almond extract. Gently stir in the combined flour mixture until just moistened. Stir in ⅔ cup of the toffee bits, followed by the pecans.

Pour into the prepared pan and bake for 25 to 30 minutes, until lightly golden. Remove from the oven and immediately sprinkle the remaining toffee bits over the top. Cool completely in the pan on a wire rack. Drizzle evenly with caramel topping before serving.

MAKES SIXTEEN 2 X 2-INCH SQUARES.

1⅓ cups all-purpose flour

½ teaspoon baking powder

¼ teaspoon salt

2 large eggs, at room temperature

½ cup sugar

½ cup firmly packed light brown sugar

⅓ cup (5⅓ tablespoons) unsalted butter, melted

1 teaspoon vanilla extract

¼ teaspoon almond extract

1 cup toffee bits, divided

½ cup coarsely chopped pecans

½ cup store-bought caramel sundae topping (your favorite brand)

Chocolate Chocolate White Chocolate Cookies

Layer upon layer of chocolate flavor baked into one stupendous cookie . . .

¾ cup all-purpose flour

½ teaspoon baking powder

½ teaspoon salt

¾ cup (1½ sticks) unsalted butter, softened

1½ cups sugar

4 large eggs, at room temperature

4 teaspoons vanilla extract

2 teaspoons instant espresso powder

4 ounces unsweetened chocolate, melted

12 ounces semisweet chocolate, melted

2 cups vanilla (or white chocolate) chips

Preheat oven to 350 degrees.

In a medium bowl, sift the flour, baking powder, and salt. Set aside.

In a large bowl, on the medium speed of an electric mixer, cream the butter and sugar until fluffy, about 2 to 3 minutes. Add the eggs, vanilla, and espresso, and beat on high speed for about 2 minutes. Turn the mixer to low and mix in the melted chocolates, stopping to scrape the bowl. Resume mixing on low speed and add the dry ingredients, mixing well. Stop the mixer and stir in the vanilla chips.

Drop by rounded teaspoonfuls onto ungreased cookie sheets, leaving several inches between for spreading. Bake for 10 to 12 minutes. Cool the cookies on the sheets for 1 minute, then remove to a rack to cool completely.

MAKES APPROXIMATELY 5 DOZEN COOKIES.

Dried Cranberry Pumpkin Bars

Preheat oven to 375 degrees.

Grease and flour a 9 x 9-inch pan.

Combine the flour, baking powder, baking soda, cinnamon, and allspice in a medium bowl. Set aside.

In a large bowl, cream the butter and sugar on the medium speed of an electric mixer until fluffy, about 2 to 3 minutes. Add the egg and incorporate. Next add in the vanilla and mix well. Then add in the pumpkin puree (at this point the mix will have a cottage-cheese-like look to it). Slowly add the combined flour mixture, beating well until combined (the mixture should now look smoother). Stir in the pecans and dried cranberries until just incorporated.

Spread the dough in the prepared pan and smooth to the edges. Bake for 25 to 35 minutes, or until a cake tester inserted into the center of the pan comes out clean. Let cool for 10 minutes before decorating with pecan halves. Allow to cool completely before cutting into bars.

MAKES NINE 3 X 3-INCH BARS.

2 cups all-purpose flour

1 teaspoon baking powder

½ teaspoon baking soda

1 teaspoon ground cinnamon

½ teaspoon ground allspice

1 cup (2 sticks) unsalted butter, softened

1 cup sugar

1 large egg, at room temperature

1 teaspoon vanilla extract

1 cup pumpkin puree

1 cup coarsely chopped pecans

1½ cups dried cranberries

Pecan halves to decorate

Drizzled Peanut Butter Chocolate Chunk Cookies

With gobs of chunky peanut butter and chocolate, a better title for this recipe might be something like "Mmmmmmm."

COOKIE INGREDIENTS:

1¼ cups all-purpose flour

½ teaspoon baking soda

½ teaspoon baking powder

¼ teaspoon salt

½ cup (1 stick) unsalted butter, softened

¾ cup chunky peanut butter

1 cup firmly packed light brown sugar

1 large egg, at room temperature

1 tablespoon vanilla extract

1 cup semisweet chocolate chunks

TOPPING INGREDIENTS:

¼ cup milk chocolate chips

Preheat oven to 350 degrees.

In a medium bowl, combine the flour, baking soda, baking powder, and salt. Set aside.

In a large bowl, cream the butter and peanut butter on the low speed of an electric mixer until smooth, about 2 to 3 minutes. Add the brown sugar and continue to beat another 1 to 2 minutes. Add the egg and vanilla and mix well. Add the dry ingredients and thoroughly mix. Stir in the chocolate chunks.

Drop by rounded teaspoonfuls onto ungreased cookie sheets, leaving 3 to 4 inches between for spreading. Bake for 10 to 12 minutes. Cool the cookies on the sheets for 1 minute, then remove to a rack to cool completely.

For the topping, place the chips into a plastic freezer bag and microwave for 1 minute on medium power, turning the bag over, and microwaving for 1 minute more. Allow to cool for about 45 seconds. Cut a tiny hole in the corner of the bag and pipe chocolate decoratively onto the cooled cookies.

MAKES 2½ TO 3 DOZEN COOKIES.

The most delicious brownies, piled high with a sweet, gooey, crunchy topping. Now that's a brownie to write home about.

Preheat oven to 350 degrees.

Grease a 9 x 13-inch baking pan.

In a medium saucepan, melt the chocolate, butter, and ¾ cup of the chocolate chips on medium heat. Stir occasionally while melting. Set aside and cool for 5 minutes.

In a medium bowl, sift the flour, baking powder, and salt. Set aside.

In a large bowl, place the eggs and whisk thoroughly. Add in the sugar and vanilla. Stir the melted ingredients into the egg mixture, mixing well. Stir in the sifted dry ingredients and mix well.

Pour the batter into the prepared pan, and even with a spatula. Bake for 25 to 30 minutes, or until a cake tester inserted into the center of the pan comes out with moist crumbs.

Remove the brownies from the oven, and immediately sprinkle the marshmallows over them. Return the pan to the oven for 3 more minutes.

While the brownies are baking, place the chocolate chips, peanut butter, and butter in a medium saucepan. Cook over low heat, stirring constantly until melted. Remove from heat, add the cereal, and mix well. Allow this to cool for 3 minutes or so. Spread the mixture evenly over the marshmallow layer. Refrigerate until chilled before cutting.

MAKES TWELVE 3 x 3–INCH BARS.

BROWNIE

INGREDIENTS:

4 ounces unsweetened chocolate

⅔ cup (1⅓ sticks) plus 1 tablespoon unsalted butter, divided

¾ cup semisweet chocolate chips

1⅓ cups all-purpose flour

1 teaspoon baking powder

½ teaspoon salt

4 large eggs, at room temperature

2 cups sugar

2 teaspoons vanilla extract

TOPPING

INGREDIENTS:

1 package (10½ ounces) mini marshmallows

1½ cups semisweet chocolate chips

1 cup smooth peanut butter

1 tablespoon unsalted butter

1½ cups crispy rice cereal

Meringues

When I was first starting out as a baker, I always thought meringues were difficult to make and had to be piped with complicated pastry bags. It is certainly not the case with these simple "kisses." Only four main ingredients and regular kitchen spoons produce these old-fashioned favorites.

2 large egg whites
½ teaspoon cream of tartar
1 teaspoon vanilla extract
⅔ cup superfine sugar

OPTIONAL:
½ cup mini chocolate chips
½ cup finely chopped walnuts
½ cup crushed peppermint candies

Preheat oven to 350 degrees.

Line 4 baking sheets with parchment paper.

Using the whisk attachment, on the low speed of a stand mixer, beat the egg whites until foamy. Add the cream of tartar and beat until fluffy (do not overbeat). Beat in the vanilla. Turn the mixer to medium, and add the sugar gradually, about 4 tablespoons at a time. Continue beating while adding the remaining sugar in batches until all of the sugar is dissolved and the meringue is very glossy. If desired, gently fold in the chips, nuts, or candies, but no more than ½ cup total.

Using 2 teaspoons, scoop a teaspoonful of meringue onto the first spoon, and push the meringue onto the lined baking sheets with the back of the second spoon, leaving about 1 inch between the cookies. Place the baking sheets in the oven and turn the oven off. Leave the cookies in the oven for at least 1 hour (even overnight), so that the cookies turn crisp.

MAKES ABOUT 4 DOZEN COOKIES.

Mint Chocolate Chocolate Chip Cookies

If you ask people to name their favorite dessert flavor combinations from childhood, mint and chocolate usually come up first. These cookies will take you to a nostalgic place with their swaths of sweet, minty icing sitting atop a perfect chocolate cookie.

Preheat oven to 350 degrees.

In a medium bowl, sift the flour, cocoa powder, baking soda, and salt. Set aside.

In a large bowl, cream the butter and both sugars on the medium speed of an electric mixer until fluffy, about 2 to 3 minutes. Add the eggs one at a time, mixing well. Then add in the vanilla. Add the sifted dry ingredients in thirds, and beat thoroughly after each addition. Then stir in the chocolate chips.

Drop by rounded teaspoonfuls onto ungreased cookie sheets, leaving 3 to 4 inches between for spreading. Bake for 8 to 10 minutes, or until slightly cracked on the surface.

Cool the cookies on the sheets for 1 minute, then remove to a rack to cool completely.

To make the glaze, mix together the sugar, water, and mint extract in a small bowl until smooth. Add a couple of drops more water if necessary for a smooth texture. Transfer the mixture into a plastic freezer storage bag, and snip off the corner. Drizzle the glaze carefully over the cooled cookies. Let the glaze set for about 10 to 15 minutes before serving.

MAKES 5 TO 6 DOZEN COOKIES.

COOKIE INGREDIENTS:

2 cups all-purpose flour

$\frac{3}{4}$ cup unsweetened cocoa powder

1 teaspoon baking soda

$\frac{1}{4}$ teaspoon salt

1 cup (2 sticks) unsalted butter, softened

1 cup firmly packed light brown sugar

$\frac{3}{4}$ cup sugar

2 large eggs, at room temperature

2 teaspoons vanilla extract

2 cups semisweet chocolate chips

GLAZE INGREDIENTS:

$1\frac{1}{2}$ cups confectioners' sugar

8 teaspoons water (a few more drops if needed)

$\frac{1}{4}$ to $\frac{1}{2}$ teaspoon peppermint extract, or more to taste

Orange Coconut Raisin Cookies

This tasty treat was my husband's idea, pure and simple. As a chef, he certainly knows his way around a good cookie. He gave me the idea for the flavors, and I produced the confection.

½ cup (1 stick) unsalted butter, softened

⅓ cup sugar

1 large egg yolk

1 cup all-purpose flour

2 teaspoons finely grated orange zest

¼ teaspoon salt

½ cup golden raisins

½ cup sweetened shredded coconut

Preheat oven to 350 degrees.

In a medium bowl, cream the butter and sugar on the medium speed of an electric mixer until fluffy, about 2 to 3 minutes. Then beat in the yolk until incorporated. Mix in the flour and blend thoroughly. Add the zest and salt. Add in the raisins and coconut, mixing until well incorporated. Remove the dough and roll into an approximate 12-inch-long by 2-inch-wide piece. Wrap in wax paper or plastic wrap and refrigerate at least 1 hour or up until overnight.

When ready to bake, cut the dough into ⅓-inch slices and place on ungreased cookie sheets, leaving 3 to 4 inches in between for spreading. Bake for 15 to 18 minutes, or until lightly golden at the edges.

Cool the cookies on the sheets for 1 minute, then remove to a rack to cool completely.

MAKES ABOUT 2 DOZEN COOKIES.

Peanut Butter Dream Bars

Preheat oven to 325 degrees.

To make the crust: In a medium bowl, combine the graham cracker crumbs with the melted butter, and then press the mixture firmly into an ungreased 9 x 13-inch pan.

Spread the pecans over the crust, then the chips, and the coconut. Pour the sweetened condensed milk evenly over the ingredients, completely covering the coconut. Use a spatula to spread if necessary.

Bake for 30 to 35 minutes, or until lightly golden. Take care not to overbake.

Allow to cool to room temperature, or overnight, before serving.

MAKES TWELVE 3 X 3-INCH BARS.

$2\frac{1}{4}$ cups graham cracker crumbs

$\frac{3}{4}$ cup ($1\frac{1}{2}$ sticks) unsalted butter, melted

1 cup coarsely chopped pecans

$\frac{1}{2}$ cup peanut butter chips

$2\frac{1}{2}$ cups sweetened, shredded coconut

2 (14-ounce) cans sweetened condensed milk

Pecan Pie Bars

My favorite pie packed into a 3-inch square. With a delightfully gooey filling laced with pecans, it doesn't get any better than this. Of course, a scoop of creamy vanilla ice cream couldn't hurt.

CRUST INGREDIENTS:

1½ cups (3 sticks) unsalted butter, softened

1 cup confectioners' sugar

3 cups all-purpose flour

1 teaspoon vanilla extract

FILLING INGREDIENTS:

3 large eggs, at room temperature

2 cups coarsely chopped pecans

1 cup sugar

1 cup light corn syrup

2 tablespoons unsalted butter, melted

1 teaspoon vanilla extract

Preheat oven to 350 degrees.

Lightly grease a 9 x 13-inch baking pan.

To make the crust: In a medium bowl, cream the butter on the low speed of an electric mixer until smooth, about 1 to 2 minutes. Add the sugar and continue creaming another minute. Add in the flour gradually, and then the vanilla, and combine until mixture resembles coarse crumbs. Form the dough into a ball. Use a large piece of wax paper to firmly and evenly press down the crust into the prepared pan. Bake the crust for 12 to 15 minutes, until lightly golden. Remove from the oven and let cool for 15 to 20 minutes before filling.

Meanwhile, make the filling: In a medium bowl, on the low speed of an electric mixer, beat the eggs well. Add the remaining ingredients and mix until incorporated. Pour the filling over the cooled crust and bake for 30 to 35 minutes, until the filling is set. When finished, allow to cool completely before cutting into bars. Run a knife around the edge of the pan before cutting into squares.

MAKES TWELVE 3 x 3-INCH BARS.

Muffins
and Quick Breads

Apple Raspberry Quick Bread

The zing of berries adds just the right touch to this warm and inviting breakfast treat.

Preheat oven to 350 degrees.

Grease and flour a 9 x 5 x 3-inch loaf pan.

In a large bowl, combine the flour, sugar, baking powder, baking soda, and salt. Set aside. In a separate bowl combine the apple juice, lemon zest, butter, and egg. Mix until well combined. Add the liquid ingredients to the dry ones and mix until just incorporated. Stir in the apples, raspberries, and walnuts, if using.

Pour the batter into the prepared pan. Bake for 55 to 65 minutes, or until a cake tester inserted into the center of the loaf comes out clean.

Let cool for 15 minutes, and serve slightly warm or at room temperature.

MAKE ONE LOAF; SERVES 8.

2 cups all-purpose flour

1 cup sugar

1½ teaspoons baking powder

½ teaspoon baking soda

1 teaspoon salt

¾ cup plus 1 tablespoon apple juice

2 teaspoons finely grated lemon zest

2 tablespoons unsalted butter, melted

1 large egg, at room temperature

1½ cups apples, peeled, cored, and chopped (approximately 2 to 3 large apples)

½ cup raspberries, fresh or frozen (thawed and drained)

½ cup walnuts (optional)

Apricot Orange Almond Muffins

Serve these warm and dripping with honey, which would be my favorite way.

2 cups all-purpose flour

1 tablespoon baking powder

½ teaspoon baking soda

¼ teaspoon salt

1 large egg, lightly beaten

1 cup buttermilk

⅔ cup firmly packed light brown sugar

½ cup (1 stick) unsalted butter, melted and slightly cooled

1 teaspoon vanilla extract

½ teaspoon almond extract

½ cup chopped dried apricots

2 tablespoons finely grated orange zest

3 to 4 tablespoons sliced almonds

Preheat oven to 400 degrees.

Thoroughly grease a muffin tin.

In a large bowl, combine the flour, baking powder, baking soda, and salt. Make a well in the center of the flour mixture. In another bowl, combine the egg, buttermilk, sugar, melted butter, vanilla, and almond extract. Once combined, stir in the apricots and zest. Add the mixture all at once to the flour mixture, and stir until just moistened. The batter may be somewhat stiff.

Spoon the batter into the prepared tin, filling each cup three-quarters full. Sprinkle each muffin with a few sliced almonds.

Bake for 16 to 20 minutes, or until a cake tester inserted into the center of a muffin comes out clean.

Cool the muffins in the pan on a wire rack for 10 minutes. Remove from the pan and serve slightly warm.

MAKES 10 TO 12 MUFFINS.

Most people's favorite muffin is blueberry. By adding bananas into the mix, I heightened the flavor and texture immensely, and the lemon zest also adds a refreshing and subtle taste.

Banana Blueberry Muffins

Preheat oven to 375 degrees.

Thoroughly grease 2 muffin tins.

In a large bowl, combine the flour, baking powder, baking soda, salt, and lemon zest. Set aside.

In a large bowl, cream the butter and brown sugar together on the medium speed of an electric mixer, about 3 minutes, until fluffy. Mix in the bananas, eggs, and apple juice. Remove the bowl from the mixer and mix in the flour mixture by hand until just moistened. In a small bowl, toss the blueberries with a couple of tablespoons of flour until just coated. Discard excess flour. Then gently fold the coated blueberries into the batter.

Spoon the batter into the prepared tins, filling each cup about three-quarters full. Bake for 18 to 22 minutes, or until a cake tester inserted into the center of a muffin comes out clean.

Cool the muffins in the pan on a wire rack for 10 minutes. Remove from the pan and serve slightly warm.

MAKES 20 TO 22 MUFFINS.

3 cups all-purpose flour, plus a few tablespoons for coating blueberries

1 teaspoon baking powder

1 teaspoon baking soda

½ teaspoon salt

2 teaspoons finely grated lemon zest

¾ cup (1½ sticks) unsalted butter, softened

1½ cups firmly packed light brown sugar

2½ cups very ripe mashed bananas (about 4 to 5 medium bananas, almost fully brown)

2 large eggs, at room temperature

¼ cup apple juice

2 cups blueberries

Buttermilk Bran Muffins

I usually think bran muffins are a bit flavorless and bland. By using cereal flakes and buttermilk to further enhance the flavor, I think you'll win the muffin popularity contest with this version of an old favorite. Try it with raisin bran cereal for a fruity variation.

3½ cups bran flakes cereal

2½ cups all-purpose flour

1 tablespoon baking soda

1½ cups sugar

1 cup warm water

2 large eggs, at room temperature

2 cups buttermilk

½ cup (1 stick) unsalted butter, melted

Preheat oven to 400 degrees.

Thoroughly grease 2 muffin tins.

In a large bowl, combine the bran flakes, flour, baking soda, and sugar. Set aside.

In a medium bowl, combine the water, eggs, and buttermilk, mixing well. Add in the melted butter. Making a well in the center of the dry ingredients, add the liquid ingredients all at once, stirring only until dry ingredients are just moistened.

Spoon the batter into the prepared tins, filling each cup about three-quarters full. Bake for 18 to 20 minutes, or until a cake tester inserted into the center of a muffin comes out with moist crumbs attached.

Cool the muffins in the pan on a wire rack for 10 minutes. Remove from the pan and serve slightly warm.

MAKES ABOUT 2 DOZEN MUFFINS.

The infusion of tea brings a light and interesting flavor to this delicious quick bread.

Cranberry Tea Loaf

Preheat oven to 350 degrees.

Grease and flour a 9 x 5 x 3-inch loaf pan.

In a small pot, bring the water and cranberry juice to a boil. Add the tea bags, cover, and brew for 5 minutes. Remove the bags and set aside to cool.

In a medium bowl, combine the flour, baking soda, and salt. Set aside.

In a large bowl, cream the butter and sugar on the low speed of an electric mixer until well blended, about 1 to 2 minutes. Add the eggs one at a time, mixing until well incorporated. Beat in the cooled tea mixture. Gradually beat in the flour mixture. Stir in the cranberries and walnuts. Pour the batter into the prepared pan, and bake 1 hour and 15 minutes, or until a cake tester inserted into the center of the loaf comes out clean.

Let cool for 15 minutes, and serve slightly warm or at room temperature.

MAKES ONE LOAF; SERVES 8.

1¼ cups water

¼ cup cranberry juice

4 regular tea bags (Lipton or brand of your choice)

3 cups all-purpose flour

1 teaspoon baking soda

½ teaspoon salt

¼ cup (½ stick) unsalted butter, softened

1 cup sugar

2 large eggs, at room temperature

1 cup chopped cranberries

1 cup chopped walnuts

Dried Cherry Poppy Seed Scones

I love the texture of scones, but they tend to be on the dry side if overbaked. Make sure you check them early to avoid this problem. Serve these warm from the oven, spread with your favorite jam.

2 cups all-purpose flour

1/3 cup sugar

2 teaspoons baking powder

1/4 teaspoon salt

1/3 cup (5 1/3 tablespoons) unsalted butter, chilled, cut into small pieces

1/2 cup heavy cream

1 large egg, lightly beaten

1 teaspoon vanilla extract

2/3 cup dried cherries

2 teaspoons finely grated orange zest

1 tablespoon poppy seeds

EGG MIXTURE:

1 large egg, lightly beaten

1 tablespoon heavy cream

Preheat oven to 375 degrees.

Line a cookie sheet with parchment paper.

In a large bowl, whisk together the flour, sugar, baking powder, and salt. Cut in the butter and blend into the flour mixture with a pastry blender or 2 forks. The mixture should look like coarse crumbs. In a small bowl, combine the heavy cream, beaten egg, and vanilla. Add this mixture to the flour mixture. Toss in the dried cherries, zest, and poppy seeds. Stir until just combined. Do not overmix.

Remove from the bowl, and knead the dough gently on a lightly floured surface. Roll or pat the dough into a circle about 7 inches in diameter and about 1 inch thick. Cut the circle into 8 triangles, like a pizza, and separate the pieces. Make a mixture of the egg and heavy cream and brush it on the scones. Place them on a cookie sheet and bake for 15 minutes, or until lightly browned.

Transfer to a wire rack to cool slightly. Serve warm.

MAKES 8 SCONES.

Pumpkin Bread

Preheat oven to 350 degrees.

Grease and flour a 9 x 3 x 5-inch loaf pan.

In a large bowl, combine the flours, baking powder, baking soda, spices, and salt. In another bowl, on the medium speed of an electric mixer, beat the pumpkin puree with the eggs, sugars, oil, and applesauce until well combined. Next mix the dry ingredients into the pumpkin mixture until thoroughly combined. Stir in the raisins.

Pour the batter into the prepared pan and bake for 50 to 55 minutes, or until a cake tester inserted into the center of the loaf comes out clean.

Let cool for 15 minutes, and serve slightly warm or at room temperature.

MAKES ONE LOAF; SERVES 8.

$1\frac{1}{2}$ cups all-purpose flour

$\frac{1}{2}$ cup whole-wheat flour

$1\frac{1}{2}$ teaspoons baking powder

1 teaspoon baking soda

2 teaspoons ground cinnamon

$\frac{1}{2}$ teaspoon ground nutmeg

$\frac{1}{4}$ teaspoon ground ginger

$\frac{1}{4}$ teaspoon salt

1 cup pumpkin puree

2 large eggs, at room temperature

$\frac{1}{2}$ cup sugar

$\frac{1}{2}$ cup firmly packed light brown sugar

$\frac{1}{4}$ cup vegetable oil

$\frac{1}{4}$ cup applesauce

1 cup raisins (golden or dark)

Whole-Wheat Orange Muffins

Consider these a wholesome and nutritious way to start the day. They taste yummiest spread with orange marmalade.

1 cup all-purpose flour

³/₄ cup whole-wheat flour

2 tablespoons wheat germ

1 tablespoon baking powder

¹/₂ teaspoon salt

¹/₂ cup milk

¹/₂ cup orange juice

¹/₃ cup honey

¹/₄ cup (¹/₂ stick) unsalted butter, softened

1 large egg, lightly beaten

2 tablespoons finely grated orange zest

³/₄ cup chopped pecans (optional)

Preheat oven to 375 degrees.

Thoroughly grease a muffin tin.

In a large bowl, sift together the flours, wheat germ, baking powder, and salt. Set aside.

In a saucepan over low heat, combine the milk, orange juice, and honey. Heat until the honey is melted, stirring occasionally. Stir in the butter and allow it to melt. Stir in the egg and zest and mix well. Remove from heat and let cool slightly.

Make a well in the center of the dry flour mixture, and pour the cooled liquid into the center. Gently stir the two together until just moistened. Gently fold in the nuts, if using. The batter may be lumpy.

Spoon the batter into the prepared tin, filling each cup about three-quarters full. Bake for 18 to 20 minutes, or until a cake tester inserted into the center of a muffin comes out clean.

Cool the muffins in the pan on a wire rack for 10 minutes. Remove from the pan and serve slightly warm.

MAKES 10 TO 12 MUFFINS.

Layer Cakes

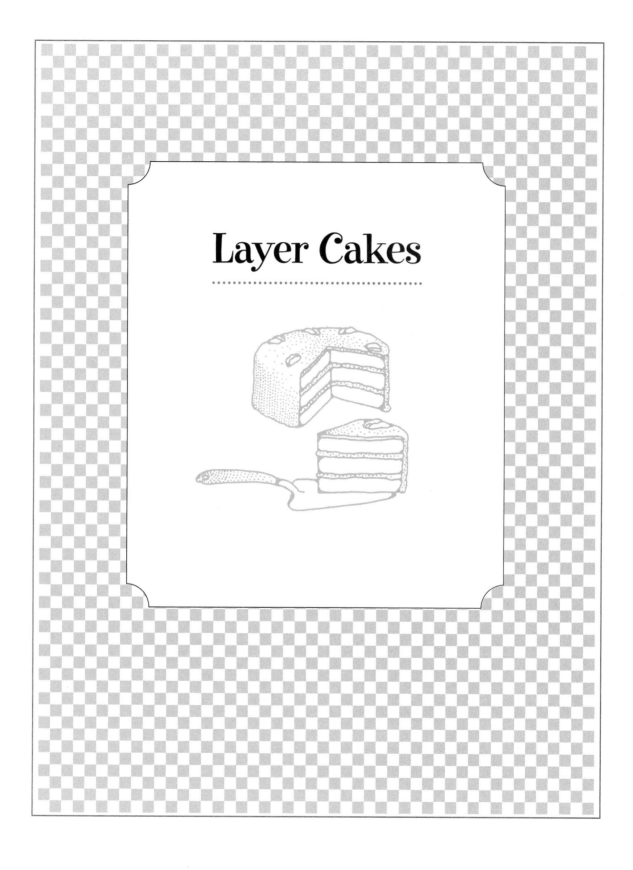

Banana Layer Cake with Chocolate Banana Liqueur Frosting

2½ cups all-purpose flour

1 teaspoon baking powder

½ teaspoon baking soda

1 teaspoon salt

⅔ cup vegetable shortening

1⅔ cups sugar

2 large eggs, at room temperature

1½ cups mashed very ripe bananas (2 to 3 medium bananas, almost fully brown)

⅔ cup buttermilk

½ cup chopped walnuts

FROSTING

1⅓ cups milk

6 tablespoons all-purpose flour

1¼ cups (2½ sticks) unsalted butter, softened

1⅓ cups sugar

½ cup unsweetened cocoa powder

1 teaspoon vanilla extract

5 tablespoons banana liqueur (or to taste)

Preheat oven to 375 degrees.

Grease and lightly flour two 9 x 2-inch round cake pans, then line the bottoms with wax paper.

In a medium bowl, combine the flour, baking powder, baking soda, and salt. Set aside.

In a large bowl, cream the shortening and sugar on the medium speed of an electric mixer until smooth, about 3 minutes. Add the eggs one at a time until well incorporated. Blend in the bananas. Add the flour mixture in two batches, alternating with the buttermilk, beating after each addition until smooth. Stir in the nuts.

Divide the batter between the prepared pans. Bake for 30 to 35 minutes, or until a cake tester inserted into the center of the cake comes out clean. Let the cakes cool in pans for 10 minutes. Remove from the pans and cool completely on a wire rack.

When the cake has cooled, frost between the layers, then the top and sides of the cake.

MAKES ONE 2-LAYER 9-INCH CAKE; SERVES 10 TO 12.

Chocolate Banana Liqueur Frosting

In a medium saucepan, whisk together the milk and flour. Cook over medium heat until thick, whisking constantly. Allow the mixture to cool. On the medium speed of an electric mixer, cream the butter and sugar for about 1 minute. Beat in the cocoa powder until thoroughly blended. Add the cooled flour mixture; then add in the vanilla and liqueur. Continue beating until fluffy and smooth.

MAKES APPROXIMATELY 4 CUPS.

Buttercup Golden Layer Cake

> *The standard by which all cakes should be measured; this foolproof cake is as wonderfully tasty as it is easy to bake. Make it as a layer cake or as cupcakes, frosted with gobs of Chocolate or Vanilla Buttercream.*

1 cup (2 sticks) unsalted butter, softened

2 cups sugar

4 large eggs, at room temperature

1 cup milk

1 teaspoon vanilla extract

1½ cups self-rising flour

1¼ cups all-purpose flour

Preheat oven to 350 degrees.

Grease and lightly flour three 9 x 2-inch round cake pans, then line the bottoms with wax paper.

In a large bowl, cream the butter and sugar on the medium speed of an electric mixer until fluffy, about 3 minutes. Add the eggs one at a time, beating well after each addition. Mix the milk and vanilla together. Thoroughly combine the flours and add in two parts, alternating with the milk and vanilla mixture and beating well after each addition.

Divide the batter between the prepared pans. Bake for 20 to 25 minutes, or until a cake tester inserted into the center of the cake comes out clean. Let the cakes cool in the pans for 10 minutes. Remove from the pans and cool completely on a wire rack.

If you're making cupcakes, line two 12-cup muffin tins with cupcake papers. Spoon the batter into the cups about two-thirds full. Bake until the tops spring back when lightly touched, about 20 to 22 minutes. Let the cupcakes cool in pans for 10 minutes. Remove the cupcakes from the pans and cool completely on a rack before icing.

When the cake has cooled, frost between the layers, then the top and sides of the cake.

MAKES ONE 3-LAYER 9-INCH CAKE AND SERVES 10 TO 12, OR APPROXIMATELY 2 DOZEN CUPCAKES.

Chocolate Buttercream

In a large bowl, beat the butter until creamy, about 2 to 3 minutes. Add the milk slowly and blend until smooth. Add the melted chocolate and beat well. Add the vanilla and beat another minute or so. Gradually add the sugar and beat until of desired consistency.

Use and store the icing at room temperature, as the icing will set if chilled. It can be stored in an airtight container for up to 3 days. This yields icing for one 2- or 3-layer 9-inch cake, or 2 dozen cupcakes.

MAKES ABOUT 4½ CUPS.

1½ cups (3 sticks) unsalted butter, softened

2 tablespoons milk

9 ounces semisweet chocolate, melted and cooled to lukewarm

1½ teaspoons vanilla extract

3 cups (or slightly more) confectioners' sugar

Vanilla Buttercream

Place the butter in a large mixing bowl. Add 4 cups of the sugar and then the milk and vanilla. Beat until smooth and creamy. Gradually add the remaining sugar, 1 cup at a time, until the icing is a good spreading consistency (you may not use all the sugar). If desired, add a few drops of food coloring, and mix thoroughly.

Use and store the icing at room temperature, as the icing will set if chilled. It can be stored in an airtight container for up to 3 days. This yields icing for one 2- or 3-layer 9-inch cake, or 2 dozen cupcakes.

MAKES ABOUT 4½ CUPS.

1 cup (2 sticks) unsalted butter, softened

7 to 8 cups confectioners' sugar

½ cup milk

2 teaspoons vanilla extract

Food coloring (optional)

Carrot Cake with Cream Cheese Icing

> *This remains my best-selling cake at the bakery, and customers still swear it's the best-tasting carrot cake they've ever eaten.*

2½ cups all-purpose flour

1 teaspoon baking powder

1 teaspoon baking soda

1 teaspoon ground cinnamon

½ teaspoon ground allspice

½ teaspoon ground ginger

1½ cups (3 sticks) unsalted butter, softened

1 cup firmly packed light brown sugar

1 cup sugar

3 large eggs, at room temperature

2 teaspoons vanilla extract

½ cup apple juice (any brand)

1½ cups peeled, grated carrots (about 3 to 4 medium carrots)

1 Golden Delicious apple, peeled, cored, and diced (about 1 cup)

1 cup finely chopped pecans

3 tablespoons heavy cream

Preheat oven to 350 degrees.

Grease and lightly flour three 9 x 2-inch round cake pans, then line the bottoms with wax paper.

In a medium bowl, combine the flour, baking powder, baking soda, and spices. Set aside.

In a large bowl, cream the butter and the sugars on the medium speed of an electric mixer until fluffy, about 3 minutes. Beat in the eggs, one at a time. Then beat in the vanilla. Add the dry ingredients in thirds to the butter mixture, alternating with the apple juice. Beat for 45 seconds after each addition, beginning and ending with the flour mixture. Stir in the carrots, apple, pecans, and cream until all the ingredients are well incorporated.

Divide the batter between the prepared pans. Bake for 30 to 35 minutes, or until a cake tester inserted into the center of the cake comes out clean. Let the cakes cool in the pans for 10 minutes. Remove from the pans and cool completely on a wire rack.*

When the cake has cooled, frost between the layers, and then the top of cake. It is not necessary to ice the sides, but you may do so if you prefer.

MAKES ONE 3-LAYER 9-INCH CAKE; SERVES 10 TO 12.

★ THESE LAYERS ARE VERY DELICATE, SO USE CARE WHEN REMOVING FROM PANS.

Cream Cheese Icing

In a large bowl, beat the cream cheese and butter on the medium speed of an electric mixer until smooth, about 2 to 3 minutes. Add the vanilla and mix well. Gradually add the sugar 1 cup at a time, and beat until desired consistency (you may not need all the sugar). Refrigerate for about 30 minutes. Allow the icing to come to room temperature before using. Refrigerate any leftovers.

This yields icing for one 3-layer 9-inch cake or 2 dozen cupcakes.

MAKES ABOUT 5 CUPS.

2 (8-ounce) packages cream cheese, softened

$\frac{1}{2}$ cup (1 stick) unsalted butter, softened

$1\frac{1}{2}$ teaspoons vanilla extract

5 to 6 cups confectioners' sugar

Devilish Chocolate Layer Cake with Brandy Whipped Cream Icing

The addition of cocoa powder to this recipe gives extra texture to the crumb of this cake, and makes for a more seductive chocolate flavor. Using a whipped cream icing balances out the "chocolatiness" in just the right way.

³⁄₄ cup unsweetened cocoa powder

2 ounces unsweetened chocolate, chopped

1¹⁄₂ cups boiling water

2¹⁄₄ cups cake flour

1¹⁄₄ cups all-purpose flour

1 teaspoon baking soda

1 teaspoon salt

1¹⁄₂ cups (3 sticks) unsalted butter, softened

1¹⁄₂ cups firmly packed light brown sugar

³⁄₄ cup sugar

4 large eggs, at room temperature

¹⁄₂ cup sour cream

2 teaspoons vanilla extract

Preheat oven to 350 degrees.

Grease and lightly flour three 9 x 2-inch round cake pans, then line the bottoms with wax paper.

In a medium bowl, combine the cocoa powder and chocolate. Pour the boiling water over the chocolate mixture and whisk until smooth. Set aside.

In another bowl, sift together the flours, baking soda, and salt. Set aside.

In a large bowl, cream the butter on the medium speed of an electric mixer for about 1 minute. Then add the sugars and beat on medium speed until fluffy, about 2 to 3 minutes. Add the eggs, one at a time, beating well after each addition. Turn the mixer to low, and add the flour mixture in thirds, alternating with the chocolate mixture, until just incorporated. Then add the sour cream and vanilla, blending until smooth.

Divide the batter between the prepared pans. Bake for 23 to 25 minutes, or until a cake tester inserted into the center of the cake comes out clean. Let the cakes cool in the pans for 10 minutes. Remove from the pans and cool completely on a wire rack.

When the cake has cooled, frost between the layers, then the top and sides of cake.

MAKES ONE 3-LAYER 9-INCH CAKE; SERVES 10 TO 12.

Brandy Whipped Cream Icing

In a large bowl, whip the heavy cream on the high speed of an electric mixer until soft peaks form. Add in the sugar and the brandy, and resume mixing on high until stiff peaks form. Use immediately to frost the completely cooled cake.

2 to 2½ cups heavy cream
¼ cup superfine sugar
3 tablespoons brandy

MAKES APPROXIMATELY 5 CUPS.

Lemon Coconut-filled White Buttermilk Cake

> *Oozing with lemony filling and topped with citrusy whipped cream, this simple vanilla cake will be considered anything but.*

CAKE INGREDIENTS:

3 cups cake flour

1 teaspoon baking soda

$\frac{1}{2}$ teaspoon salt

1 cup (2 sticks) unsalted butter, softened

2 cups sugar, divided

1 cup buttermilk

2 teaspoons vanilla extract

$\frac{1}{2}$ teaspoon almond extract

6 large egg whites

1 teaspoon cream of tartar

FILLING INGREDIENTS:

2 large egg yolks

$\frac{2}{3}$ cup sugar

2 tablespoons cornstarch

$\frac{1}{2}$ cup water

1 tablespoon lemon juice

1 tablespoon unsalted butter

$\frac{3}{4}$ cup sweetened, shredded coconut, toasted*

1 teaspoon finely grated lemon zest

Preheat oven to 350 degrees.

To make the cake: Grease and lightly flour three 9 x 2-inch round cake pans, then line the bottoms with wax paper.

In a medium bowl, sift together the flour, baking soda, and salt. Set aside.

In a large bowl, on the medium speed of an electric mixer, cream the butter and $1\frac{1}{3}$ cups of the sugar until light and fluffy, about 2 to 3 minutes. Add the flour mixture in three parts, alternating with the buttermilk. Blend in the vanilla and almond extracts.

In another bowl, beat the egg whites at medium speed until foamy. Add the cream of tartar and beat until soft peaks form. Gradually add the remaining sugar, then turn the mixer up to medium-high, beating until stiff peaks form. Gently fold the mixture into the batter, making sure no streaks of whites are showing.

Divide the batter between the prepared pans. Bake for 25 to 30 minutes, or until a cake tester inserted into the center of the cake comes out clean. Let the cakes cool in the pans for 10 minutes. Remove from the pans and cool completely on a wire rack.

To make the filling: In a small bowl, beat the egg yolks and set aside. In a medium saucepan, whisk together the sugar and cornstarch. Over medium heat, stir in the water and lemon juice until the mixture is smooth. Bring to a boil, stirring constantly. Lower the heat and simmer for 2 to 3 minutes, until the mixture thickens and turns glossy, stirring occasionally. Slowly pour half of the lemon mixture over the egg yolks and whisk to combine. Pour the egg mixture back into the saucepan and cook over low heat, stirring constantly, until the mixture thickens some more. Remove from the heat, and stir in the butter, coconut, and zest until well incorporated. Let cool to room temperature before using.

To make the frosting: In a large bowl, whip the heavy cream on the high speed of an electric mixer until soft peaks form. Add in the sugar, juice, and zest, and mix on high until stiff peaks form.

When the cake has cooled, fill the cake between the layers, then frost the top and sides of cake. Garnish with shredded coconut, if desired.

MAKES ONE 3-LAYER 9-INCH CAKE; SERVES 10 TO 12.

★ NOTE: TO TOAST THE COCONUT, SPREAD OUT EVENLY ON A BAKING SHEET AND PLACE IN A PREHEATED 325-DEGREE OVEN FOR 3 TO 5 MINUTES. SHAKE THE PAN ABOUT HALFWAY THROUGH TO INSURE EVEN COLOR. IT'S DONE WHEN THE COCONUT IS A RICH GOLDEN COLOR AND QUITE FRAGRANT.

FROSTING

INGREDIENTS:

2 cups heavy cream

$\frac{1}{4}$ cup superfine sugar

2 tablespoons fresh lemon juice

1 teaspoon finely grated lemon zest

GARNISH:

Sweetened, shredded coconut

Lord Baltimore Cake with White Mountain Frosting

The beautiful and elegant Lady Baltimore was a hit in my first Buttercup cookbook, gracing the back cover. Its lovely partner is featured here, with my own particular versions of filling and frosting. Lord Baltimore is usually made as a typical yellow cake, meaning only egg yolks are included, but I prefer whole eggs for a much moister cake. Be sure to make the frosting before the filling, since you'll use some in the filling recipe as well.

CAKE INGREDIENTS:

2½ cups cake flour

2 teaspoons baking powder

½ teaspoon salt

1 cup (2 sticks) unsalted butter, softened

2 cups sugar

4 large eggs, at room temperature

1 cup milk

2 teaspoons vanilla extract

WHITE MOUNTAIN FROSTING

INGREDIENTS:

3 large egg whites

1½ teaspoons vanilla extract

½ cup cold water

1½ cups sugar

¼ plus ⅛ teaspoon cream of tartar

Pinch salt

Preheat oven to 350 degrees.

Grease and lightly flour three 9 x 2-inch round cake pans, then line the bottoms with wax paper.

To make the cake: In a medium bowl, sift the flour, baking powder, and salt together and set aside.

In a large bowl, cream the butter and sugar on the medium speed of an electric mixer until fluffy, about 3 minutes. Add the eggs one at a time, mixing well after each addition. Combine the milk and vanilla in a measuring cup. Add half of the flour mixture to the butter mixture, followed by half of the combined milk and vanilla, mixing well on low speed. Add the remaining flour and liquid, and mix until smooth.

Divide the batter between the prepared pans. Bake for 20 to 25 minutes, or until a cake tester inserted into the center of the cake comes out clean. Let the cakes cool in the pans for 10 minutes. Remove from the pans and cool completely on a wire rack.

To make the frosting: In a standing mixer bowl, combine the egg whites and vanilla and set aside. In a heavy-bottomed saucepan, over high heat, combine the water with the sugar, cream of tartar, and salt. When the mixture begins to bubble at edges, stir once to make sure the sugar is dissolved completely, then let it come to a rolling boil (about 2 to 3 minutes) and remove immediately from the heat.

Meanwhile, on medium speed, beat the egg whites and vanilla with the whisk attachment until foamy, about 1 minute.

Without turning off the mixer, pour the sugar syrup into the beaten egg whites in a thin, steady stream. Turn the mixer up to medium-high and continue beating constantly for about 5 minutes or until stiff peaks form but frosting is still creamy and glossy.

To make the filling: In a medium bowl, combine all ingredients but the frosting until well mixed. Combine about 1 to $1\frac{1}{2}$ cups of the White Mountain Frosting with the filling mixture, saving the remainder for frosting the outside and top of the cake.

When the cake has cooled, spread half the filling between the first two layers of the cake, then the other half between the second and third layers. Then use the remaining frosting to frost the top and outside of the cake. Garnish with halved figs and pecans, if desired.

MAKES ONE 3-LAYER 9-INCH CAKE; SERVES 10 TO 12.

★ NOTE: THIS CAKE IS BEST WHEN SERVED THE DAY IT IS FILLED AND FROSTED.

FILLING INGREDIENTS:

$\frac{1}{2}$ cup almond macaroon cookie crumbs

$\frac{1}{2}$ cup finely chopped pecans

$\frac{1}{4}$ cup finely chopped almonds

$\frac{1}{4}$ cup quartered maraschino cherries

$\frac{1}{4}$ cup finely chopped figs

2 tablespoons fresh orange juice

1 teaspoon grated orange zest

1 to $1\frac{1}{2}$ cups White Mountain Frosting (see opposite page)

GARNISH:

Halved dried figs

Coarsely chopped pecans

Orange Almond Layer Cake with Creamy Vanilla Frosting

Although a food processor and a mixer are necessary for this recipe, don't be put off by the equipment. The taste and texture of this cake are so incredible, the effort is well worth it.

3 large oranges

2 cups plus 1 tablespoon sugar

2 cups all-purpose flour

1 cup whole almonds, blanched

2 teaspoons baking powder

$\frac{1}{2}$ teaspoon salt

1 cup (2 sticks) unsalted butter, softened

4 large eggs, at room temperature

1 cup milk

$\frac{1}{2}$ teaspoon vanilla extract

$\frac{1}{4}$ teaspoon almond extract

GARNISH:
Whole almonds
Orange slices

Preheat oven to 350 degrees.

Grease and lightly flour three 9 x 2-inch round cake pans, then line the bottoms with wax paper.

Using a coarse grater, zest the oranges until $\frac{1}{2}$ cup of zest is measured. Reserve the oranges for later juicing. Place the zest plus 2 cups of sugar in a food processor and blend until finely textured. Set the sugar mixture aside. Clean out the processor for the next step.

Place the flour, almonds, baking powder, and salt in the processor. Blend until finely ground and set aside.

In a large bowl, on the medium speed of an electric mixer, beat the butter until smooth. Add the sugar mixture and beat until fluffy, about 2 to 3 minutes. Beat in the eggs one at a time. Mix the milk and both extracts in a measuring cup. Turning the mixer to low, beat in the flour mixture in two parts, alternating with the milk mixture, blending thoroughly.

Divide the batter between the prepared pans. Bake for 22 to 25 minutes, or until a cake tester inserted into the center of the cake comes out clean. Let the cakes cool in the pans for 10 minutes. Remove from the pans and cool completely on a wire rack.

Meanwhile, juice the oranges and reserve $1\frac{1}{2}$ cups fresh orange juice. Combine the juice and the remaining tablespoon of sugar in a small saucepan and cook until reduced to $\frac{1}{2}$ cup, about 5 minutes. Brush the warm juice mixture over the tops of the cooled cake layers.

Creamy Vanilla Frosting

In a heavy-bottomed saucepan, combine the flour and milk, blending thoroughly. Cook over medium heat until thickened, stirring constantly. Remove from the heat and set aside to cool for 10 minutes or so. In a medium bowl, on the medium speed of an electric mixer, beat the shortening and butter until creamy. Add the sugar and beat until light and fluffy. Add in the vanilla. Then beat in the flour mixture, beating until smooth and of desired consistency.

When the cake has cooled, fill between the layers (syrup side up), then frost the top and sides of cake. Garnish with almonds and orange slices, if desired.

MAKES ONE 3-LAYER 9-INCH CAKE; SERVES 10 TO 12.

$\frac{1}{2}$ cup plus 2 tablespoons all-purpose flour

1 cup milk

$\frac{1}{2}$ cup vegetable shortening

$\frac{1}{2}$ cup (1 stick) unsalted butter, softened

1$\frac{1}{4}$ cups sugar

1 teaspoon vanilla extract

Our Favorite Chocolate Layer Cake

Many of my customers ask me why their chocolate cupcakes don't taste the same at home as they do from the bakery, using the "Over-the-Top" Chocolate Layer Cake recipe from my first Buttercup cookbook. That's because it's not the one we make about 25 to 30 batches of every day; if you're looking for your favorite chocolate cupcake just as we make it in the bakery, here it is. Make it as cupcakes or as a 2- or 3-layer cake; just be sure to adjust the baking time slightly depending on the number of layers you're making.

2 cups all-purpose flour

1 teaspoon baking soda

½ teaspoon salt

1 cup (2 sticks) unsalted butter, softened

1 cup sugar

1 cup firmly packed light brown sugar

4 large eggs, at room temperature

6 ounces unsweetened chocolate, melted

¾ cup buttermilk

1 teaspoon vanilla extract

¼ cup sour cream

Preheat oven to 350 degrees.

Grease and lightly flour two or three 9 x 2-inch round cake pans, then line the bottoms with wax paper.

In a medium bowl, sift together the flour, baking soda, and salt. Set aside.

In a large bowl, cream the butter and the sugars on the medium speed of an electric mixer until fluffy, about 2 to 3 minutes. Add the eggs one at a time, beating well after each addition. Add the chocolate, mixing until well incorporated. Add the dry ingredients in thirds, alternating with the buttermilk and vanilla, beating after each addition until smooth. Stir in the sour cream.

Divide the batter between the prepared pans. Bake for 25 to 30 minutes, or until a cake tester inserted into the center of the cake comes out clean. Let the cakes cool in the pans for 10 minutes. Remove from the pans and cool completely on a wire rack.

If you're making cupcakes, line two 12-cup muffin tins with cupcake papers. Spoon the batter into the cups to about two-thirds full. Bake until the tops spring back when lightly touched, about 20 to 22 minutes. Let the cupcakes cool in the pans for 10 minutes. Remove the cupcakes from the pans and cool completely on a rack before icing.

When the cake has cooled, frost between the layers, then the top and sides of the cake. Frost with either Chocolate or Vanilla Butter-cream (page 35).

MAKES ONE 2- OR 3-LAYER 9-INCH CAKE AND SERVES 8 TO 10,
OR APPROXIMATELY 2 DOZEN CUPCAKES.

Cupcakes, Cupcakes, Cupcakes . . .

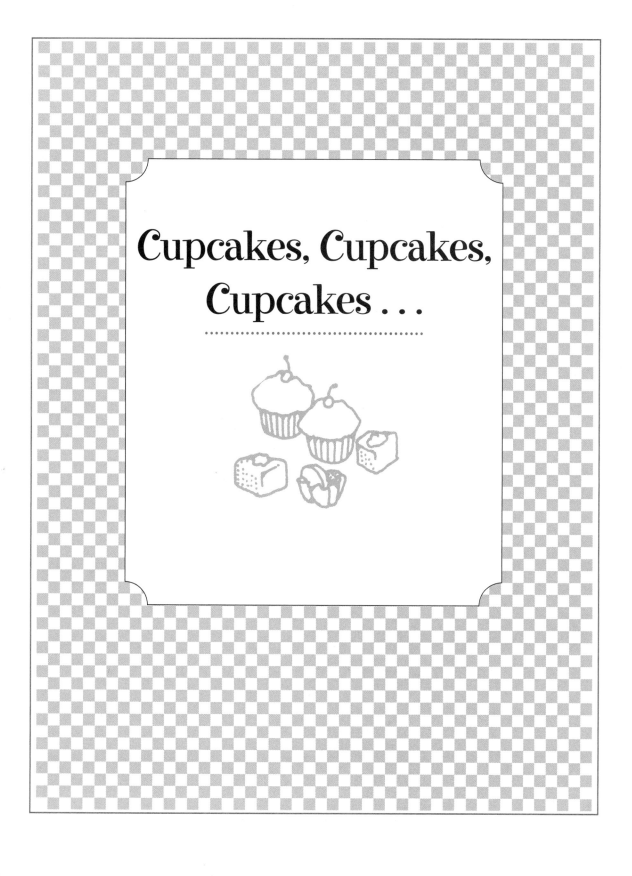

Black and White Cupcakes

Preheat oven to 350 degrees.

Line 2 muffin tins with cupcake papers.

In a medium bowl, beat the cream cheese, egg, and $\frac{1}{3}$ cup of sugar on the medium speed of an electric mixer until light and fluffy, about 2 minutes. Stir in the chocolate chips and set aside.

In a large bowl, thoroughly combine the flour, the remaining cup of sugar, cocoa powder, baking soda, and salt. Make a well in the center of the dry ingredients and add the water, oil, vinegar, and vanilla. Mix the wet and dry ingredients until just blended.

Fill each muffin cup one-third full with the cocoa batter, then top with a spoonful of the cream cheese mixture until the paper is about two-thirds full. Bake 25 to 30 minutes, or until the tops spring back when lightly touched. Let the cupcakes cool in the pans for 10 minutes. Remove from the pans and cool completely on a wire rack.

MAKES 18 TO 20 CUPCAKES.

1 (8-ounce) package cream cheese, softened

1 large egg, at room temperature

$1\frac{1}{3}$ cups sugar, divided

1 cup miniature semisweet chocolate chips

$1\frac{1}{2}$ cups all-purpose flour

$\frac{1}{4}$ cup unsweetened cocoa powder

1 teaspoon baking soda

$\frac{1}{2}$ teaspoon salt

1 cup warm water

$\frac{1}{3}$ cup vegetable oil

1 tablespoon apple cider vinegar

1 teaspoon vanilla extract

Chunky Monkey Cupcakes

My daughter, Isabel, is just crazy for bananas. Since she's still little, I bake these for her without the icing. For the grown-ups in the house, I frost them with Chocolate Buttercream (page 35) or Chocolate Banana Liqueur Frosting (page 33).

3 cups cake flour

1 teaspoon ground nutmeg

1 teaspoon baking soda

1/2 teaspoon salt

1 1/2 cups vegetable oil

2 cups sugar

3 large eggs, at room temperature

1 teaspoon vanilla extract

2 cups mashed very ripe bananas (about 3 to 4 medium bananas, almost fully brown)

1/4 cup applesauce

2/3 cups milk

1 cup semisweet chocolate chunks

Preheat oven to 325 degrees.

Line 3 muffin tins with cupcake papers.

In a small bowl, combine the flour, nutmeg, baking soda, and salt. Set aside.

In a medium bowl, beat the oil and sugar on the medium speed of an electric mixer until smooth, about 1 to 2 minutes. Beat in the eggs one at a time; then add the vanilla. Add in the bananas and applesauce, blending thoroughly. Add the dry ingredients in thirds, alternating with the milk, until well combined. Stir in the chocolate chunks.

Spoon the batter into the cups to about two-thirds full. Bake for 22 to 24 minutes, or until the tops spring back when lightly touched. Let the cupcakes cool in the pans for 10 minutes. Remove from the pans and cool completely on a wire rack.

MAKES ABOUT 2 1/2 DOZEN CUPCAKES.

Cranberry Cupcakes with Maple Cream Cheese Icing

Preheat oven to 350 degrees.

Line a muffin tin with cupcake papers.

In a medium bowl, sift the flour, baking powder, cinnamon, and salt. Set aside.

In another bowl, cream the butter and sugar together on the medium speed of an electric mixer until fluffy, about 1 to 2 minutes. Add in the eggs, one at a time, and then the vanilla, beating well. Add in the dry ingredients, alternating with the milk, in two separate additions. Stir in the cranberries.

Spoon the batter into the cups to about two-thirds full. Bake for 20 to 22 minutes, or until the tops spring back when lightly touched. Let the cupcakes cool in the pan for 10 minutes. Remove from the pan and cool completely on a wire rack.

MAKES 12 CUPCAKES.

$1\frac{1}{2}$ cups all-purpose flour

1 teaspoon baking powder

$\frac{1}{2}$ teaspoon ground cinnamon

$\frac{1}{4}$ teaspoon salt

$\frac{1}{2}$ cup (1 stick) unsalted butter, softened

$\frac{2}{3}$ cup sugar

2 large eggs, at room temperature

$\frac{1}{2}$ teaspoon vanilla extract

4 tablespoons milk

1 cup fresh cranberries, coarsely chopped

Maple Cream Cheese Icing

1 (8-ounce) package cream cheese, softened

$\frac{1}{4}$ cup ($\frac{1}{2}$ stick) unsalted butter, softened

10 tablespoons pure maple syrup

$\frac{1}{2}$ teaspoon maple extract (or more to taste)

In a large bowl, beat the cream cheese and butter on the medium speed of an electric mixer until smooth, about 2 to 3 minutes. Gradually add the maple syrup, and then the extract, and beat until well incorporated. Refrigerate for 1 hour. Remove from the refrigerator 5 to 10 minutes before using. Spread onto the completely cool cupcakes.

MAKES ABOUT 1$\frac{1}{2}$ CUPS (ENOUGH TO FROST 12 CUPCAKES).

German Chocolate Cupcakes with Caramel Pecan Frosting

> *Whenever my sister Sharon is on a diet, her worst fear is my bringing over her absolute favorite cupcakes. She'll hem and haw, and invariably give in to eating "just one." You might have to break your diet for one of these, too.*

1 package (4 ounces) Baker's German's Sweet Chocolate, broken into squares

$\frac{1}{2}$ cup water

2 cups all-purpose flour

$1\frac{1}{2}$ teaspoons baking soda

$\frac{1}{4}$ teaspoon salt

4 large eggs, separated

1 cup (2 sticks) unsalted butter, softened

2 cups sugar

1 teaspoon vanilla extract

1 cup buttermilk

Preheat oven to 350 degrees.

Line 3 muffin tins with cupcake papers.

In a small saucepan over low heat, combine the chocolate with the water, stirring to melt the chocolate completely. Set aside to cool for 10 minutes.

Meanwhile, in a medium bowl, sift together the flour, baking soda, and salt. Set aside.

In a small bowl, lightly beat the egg yolks.

In a large bowl, cream the butter and sugar on the medium speed of an electric mixer until light and fluffy, about 3 minutes. Add the egg yolks, beating until well combined. Add in the chocolate mixture and the vanilla extract. Add the dry ingredients in thirds, alternating with the buttermilk, beating after each addition until smooth. In a separate bowl, beat the egg whites on the high speed of an electric mixer until soft peaks form. Gently fold into the batter until no streaks of white are showing.

Spoon the batter into the cups to about two-thirds full. Bake for 23 to 25 minutes, or until the tops spring back when lightly touched. Be careful not to overbake, as this cake has a lighter texture than most. Let the cupcakes cool in the pans for 10 minutes. Remove from the pans and cool completely on a wire rack. Spread on Caramel Pecan Frosting (page 56).

MAKES ABOUT 2½ TO 3 DOZEN CUPCAKES.

Caramel Pecan Frosting

1½ cans (18 ounces) evaporated milk

6 large egg yolks

2 cups sugar

1 cup (2 sticks) cold unsalted butter, cut into small pieces

2 teaspoons vanilla extract

4 cups sweetened shredded coconut

2 cups coarsely chopped pecans

In a large pot, whisk together the evaporated milk and egg yolks. Stir in the sugar, butter, and vanilla extract. Stir continuously over medium heat about 10 to 12 minutes, or until thickened and bubbly and golden in color. Remove from the heat. Stir in the coconut and pecans. Transfer to a large bowl and cool until room temperature and of good spreading consistency (about 2 hours; the frosting will thicken as it cools).

Spread the frosting over tops of completely cooled cupcakes.

Gingerbread Cupcakes with Pumpkin Cream Cheese Icing

Nothing smells as fragrant as gingerbread baking in the oven. I created these cupcakes with that country kitchen scent in mind. The icing is impossibly good spread on top of these cupcakes.

Preheat oven to 350 degrees.

Line 2 muffin tins with cupcake papers.

In a medium bowl, combine the flour, baking soda, salt, and spices. Set aside.

In a large bowl, cream the butter and brown sugar on the medium speed of an electric mixer until fluffy, about 2 to 3 minutes. Beat in the eggs one at a time. Add the dry ingredients in two parts, alternating with the buttermilk. Stir in the molasses and vanilla.

Spoon the batter into the cups to about two-thirds full. Bake 20 to 25 minutes, or until the tops spring back when lightly touched. Let the cupcakes cool in the pans for 10 minutes. Remove from the pans and cool completely on a wire rack.

MAKES 24 CUPCAKES.

Pumpkin Cream Cheese Icing

In a large bowl, beat the cream cheese and pumpkin on the medium speed of an electric mixer until smooth, about 2 to 3 minutes. Add the spices, zest, and vanilla extract and mix well. Gradually add the sugar and beat until desired consistency (you may not need all the sugar). Refrigerate for 1 hour. Remove from refrigerator 5 to 10 minutes before using. Spread on the tops of the completely cool cupcakes.

MAKES ABOUT 2 CUPS (ENOUGH TO FROST 24 CUPCAKES).

3 cups all-purpose flour

1 teaspoon baking soda

1/2 teaspoon salt

1 1/2 teaspoons ground ginger

1 teaspoon ground cinnamon

1/2 teaspoon ground allspice

1 cup (2 sticks) unsalted butter, softened

1 cup firmly packed light brown sugar

4 large eggs, at room temperature

1 cup buttermilk

2 tablespoons light, unsulfured molasses

2 teaspoons vanilla extract

ICING:

1 (8-ounce) package cream cheese, softened

1/2 cup pumpkin puree

1/2 teaspoon ground allspice

1/4 teaspoon ground nutmeg

1 tablespoon finely grated orange zest

1/2 teaspoon vanilla extract

3 1/2 to 4 cups confectioners' sugar

Milky Way Cupcakes

My all-time favorite candy bar baked into a cupcake: it's a pretty yummy combination.

3 medium-size, classic Milky Way candy bars, cut up

½ cup (1 stick) unsalted butter, softened, divided

1¼ cups all-purpose flour

½ teaspoon baking soda

1 cup sugar

2 large eggs, at room temperature

½ cup plus 2 tablespoons buttermilk

Preheat oven to 350 degrees.

Line 2 muffin tins with cupcake papers.

In a medium saucepan, melt the candy bars with ½ stick butter over low heat. Stir occasionally until smooth and set aside. Cool slightly.

In a small bowl, whisk together the flour and baking soda. Set aside.

In a large bowl, cream the sugar and the remaining ½ stick of butter on the medium speed of an electric mixer until fluffy, about 1 to 2 minutes. Add the eggs one at a time, beating until well incorporated. Add the dry ingredients alternating with the buttermilk, beginning and ending with the flour mixture. Stir in the melted candy (which should still be warm), mixing thoroughly.

Spoon the batter into the cups to about two-thirds full. Bake for 20 to 22 minutes, or until the tops spring back when lightly touched. Let the cupcakes cool in the pans for 10 minutes. Remove from the pans and cool completely on a wire rack.

Frost with Chocolate Buttercream (page 35), White Mountain Frosting (page 42), or Caramel Pecan Frosting (page 56).

MAKES 15 TO 16 CUPCAKES.

Peanut Butter and Jelly Cupcakes with Chunky Peanut Butter Frosting

When experimenting with these at the bakery, my staff went wide-eyed with delight after tasting them—now <u>that's</u> a compliment!

Preheat oven to 350 degrees.

Line 2 muffin tins with cupcake papers.

In a medium bowl, sift the flour, baking powder, and salt. Set aside.

In a large bowl, cream the butter and sugar on the medium speed of an electric mixer until fluffy, about 2 to 3 minutes. Add the eggs one at a time, beating until well incorporated. Add the dry ingredients in two parts, alternating with the milk. Add in the vanilla.

Spoon the batter into the cups to about two-thirds full. Bake for 20 to 22 minutes, or until the tops spring back when lightly touched. Let the cupcakes cool in the pans for 10 minutes. Remove from the pans and cool completely on a wire rack.

When the cupcakes are thoroughly cool, fill a squeeze bottle with jelly, and then insert the tip of the bottle into the center of the cooled cupcake. Carefully squeeze about 1 tablespoon into the center of each cupcake, being careful not to let too much jelly ooze out of the top. Frost with Chunky Peanut Butter Frosting (page 60), and garnish with roasted salted peanuts or crushed peanut butter cups.

MAKES 12 TO 14 CUPCAKES.

1½ cups all-purpose flour

1 teaspoon baking powder

½ teaspoon salt

½ cup (1 stick) unsalted butter, softened

1 cup sugar

2 large eggs, at room temperature

¾ cup milk

2 teaspoons vanilla extract

Approximately 1 cup grape jelly

GARNISH:

Coarsely chopped peanuts or crushed peanut butter cups

Chunky Peanut Butter Frosting

¼ cup (½ stick) unsalted
   butter, softened

¾ cup chunky peanut butter

4 ounces cream cheese,
   softened

2 cups confectioners' sugar

½ tablespoon milk (a few
   drops more if needed)

In a large bowl, beat the butter, peanut butter, and cream cheese on the medium speed of an electric mixer until light and fluffy, about 1 to 2 minutes. On low speed, slowly add 1 cup of the sugar, then a few drops of milk. Then turn the mixer up to medium-high to thoroughly mix. Add the remaining sugar and a few more drops of milk if necessary. Mix on high speed until fluffy and good spreading consistency. Use immediately.

MAKES ABOUT 2½ CUPS (ENOUGH TO FROST 14 CUPCAKES).

Splenda-iferous Cream-Filled Vanilla Cupcakes

2¼ cups cake flour

½ cup instant nonfat powdered milk

2 teaspoons baking powder

½ teaspoon baking soda

¼ teaspoon salt

¾ cup (1½ sticks) unsalted butter, softened

½ cup Splenda Sugar Blend for Baking

3 large eggs, at room temperature

1 cup buttermilk

2 teaspoons vanilla extract

Preheat oven to 350 degrees.

Line 2 muffin tins with cupcake papers.

In a medium bowl, combine the flour, powdered milk, baking powder, baking soda, and salt. Set aside.

In a large bowl, cream the butter and Splenda on the medium speed of an electric mixer until fluffy, about 2 to 3 minutes. Add the eggs one at a time, beating until well incorporated. Add the dry ingredients in two parts, alternating with the buttermilk. Add in the vanilla and mix well.

Spoon the batter into the cups to about two-thirds full. Bake for 18 to 20 minutes, or until a cake tester inserted into the center of the cupcakes comes out clean. Let the cupcakes cool in the pans for 10 minutes. Remove from the pans and cool completely on a wire rack.

Follow the instructions for Vanilla Filling and Frosting (page 62).

When the cupcakes are thoroughly cool, fill a squeeze bottle with the filling, and then insert the tip of the bottle into the center of the cooled cupcake. Carefully squeeze about 1 tablespoon into the center of each cupcake, being careful not to let too much ooze out of the top. When done, frost the tops of the cupcakes.

MAKES 18 CUPCAKES.

Vanilla Filling and Frosting

2 cups (4 sticks) unsalted
butter, cut into small
pieces, divided

1 cup Splenda Sugar Blend
for Baking, divided

1 tablespoon plus 1 teaspoon
vanilla extract, divided

1 cup half-and-half, divided

In a medium saucepan, place 2 sticks of butter, $\frac{1}{2}$ cup of Splenda, and 1 tablespoon of vanilla. Melt slowly over low heat, stirring occasionally. Allow to cool for 10 minutes. Transfer the mixture to a large bowl, and using the whisk attachment of a stand mixer, whip this mixture at high speed until the ingredients start to become stiff. Add to that $\frac{1}{2}$ cup half-and-half, 2 more sticks butter, $\frac{1}{2}$ cup Splenda, and 1 teaspoon vanilla. Whip again for 1 to 2 minutes, and add the remaining $\frac{1}{2}$ cup of half-and-half. Continue whipping on medium-high speed until stiff peaks form.

MAKES APPROXIMATELY 4 CUPS.

Coffee Cakes,
Tube Cakes,
and Pound Cakes

Amaretto Cake

Preheat oven to 350 degrees.

Grease and flour a 10-inch Bundt pan.

In a medium bowl, combine the flour with the baking powder and set aside.

In a large bowl, cream the butter and sugar on the medium speed of an electric mixer until fluffy, about 3 minutes. Add the eggs one at a time, mixing well after each addition. Combine the milk, almond extract, and ¾ cup of amaretto in a measuring cup. Add half of the flour to the butter mixture, followed by half of the combined liquid, mixing well on low speed, then add the remaining flour and combined liquid, until thoroughly mixed. Fold in the ground almonds.

Pour the batter into the prepared pan and bake for 1 hour, or until a cake tester inserted into the center of the cake comes out clean.

Cool the cake in the pan for 15 minutes. Poke some holes into the cake with a sharp knife, then pour the remaining ¼ cup of amaretto over the warm cake. Let it soak in for about another 15 minutes, and then invert cake onto a plate to cool completely.

If desired, whip the heavy cream and the additional 2 tablespoons of amaretto until soft peaks form, and spoon over slices of cake.

SERVES 12 TO 16.

4 cups all-purpose flour

2 teaspoons baking powder

2 cups (4 sticks) unsalted butter, softened

3 cups sugar

6 large eggs, at room temperature

¾ cup milk

1 teaspoon almond extract

1 cup amaretto liqueur (divided)

2 cups ground almonds

¾ cup heavy cream (optional)

2 tablespoons amaretto liqueur (optional)

Apricot Coconut Date Pound Cake

The addition of coconut milk to this recipe makes this one of the moistest cakes you'll ever taste; fill it with your favorite dried fruits if you like, instead of the apricots and dates that I love.

3 cups all-purpose flour

1 teaspoon baking soda

1/2 teaspoon salt

2 cups (4 sticks) unsalted butter, softened

3 cups sugar

6 large eggs, at room temperature

2 teaspoons vanilla extract

1/2 cup coconut milk (not cream of coconut)

1/2 cup sour cream

1 cup sweetened, shredded coconut

3/4 cup chopped dried apricots

1/2 cup chopped dates

Preheat oven to 325 degrees.

Grease and flour a 10-inch tube pan or kugelhopf pan (a plain Bundt pan is fine, too).

In a medium bowl, combine the flour, baking soda, and salt. Set aside.

In a large bowl, cream the butter and sugar on the medium speed of an electric mixer until fluffy, about 2 to 3 minutes. Add the eggs one at a time. Then add the vanilla. Stop and scrape the bowl. Resume mixing and add the dry ingredients in two parts, alternating with the coconut milk, beating after each addition until smooth. Stir in the sour cream until thoroughly combined. Then mix in the coconut, apricots, and dates.

Pour the batter into the prepared pan and bake for 1 hour and 20 minutes, or until a cake tester inserted into the center of the cake comes out clean.

Let the cake cool in the pan for 15 minutes. Remove from the pan and cool completely on a wire rack.

SERVES 12 TO 16.

Peach Pandowdy

Lemon Coconut-Filled White Buttermilk Cake

Butterscotch Pudding

*Peanut Butter and Jelly Cupcakes
with Chunky Peanut Butter Frosting*

Mississippi Mud Cake

Dried Cherry Poppy Seed Scones

Lime Cheesecake with Gingersnap Crust

CLOCKWISE FROM LEFT: *Marshmallow Crunch Brownie Bars, Drizzled Peanut Butter Chocolate Chunk Cookies, Orange Coconut Raisin Cookies*

Banana Oatmeal Crumb Cake

Coffee cakes are so great at breakfasttime, for a midmorning pick-me-up, or as an afternoon treat with a cold glass of milk. Not only is this cake wonderfully light, but the topping will melt in your mouth.

Preheat oven to 350 degrees.

Grease and lightly flour an 8 x 8-inch baking pan.

For the cake: In a medium bowl, combine the flour, oats, baking soda, and salt. Set aside.

In a large bowl, cream the butter and brown sugar on the medium speed of an electric mixer until light and fluffy, about 3 minutes. Beat in the eggs one at a time until well combined. Next, beat in the bananas and vanilla. Add the flour mixture, beating until well combined. Pour the batter into the prepared pan and set aside.

For the topping: In a medium bowl, combine the rolled oats, brown sugar, melted butter, and cinnamon together until crumbly. Generously sprinkle the cake with the topping mixture.

Bake for 35 to 40 minutes, or until a cake tester inserted into the center of the cake comes out clean.

Let cool for 20 to 30 minutes and serve directly from the pan.

SERVES 10 TO 12.

CAKE INGREDIENTS:

$\frac{3}{4}$ cup all-purpose flour

$1\frac{1}{3}$ cups rolled oats (not quick-cooking oats)

1 teaspoon baking soda

$\frac{1}{2}$ teaspoon salt

$\frac{1}{2}$ cup (1 stick) unsalted butter, softened

$\frac{2}{3}$ cup firmly packed light brown sugar

2 large eggs, at room temperature

1 cup very ripe mashed bananas (about 2 small bananas, almost fully brown)

1 teaspoon vanilla extract

TOPPING INGREDIENTS:

$\frac{3}{4}$ cup rolled oats

$\frac{1}{3}$ cup firmly packed light brown sugar

2 tablespoons butter, melted and cooled

$\frac{1}{2}$ teaspoon ground cinnamon

Chocolate Angel Food Cake

Here's a wonderful variation to the perfect fat-free dessert. With nary a fat molecule in sight, you'll want to cheat a little: Pour some chocolate sauce over a big slice and indulge.

¾ *cup cake flour*

¼ *cup unsweetened cocoa powder*

1½ *cups sugar, divided*

13 *or* 14 *large egg whites (should equal 2 cups)*

1½ *teaspoons cream of tartar*

1 *teaspoon vanilla extract*

¼ *teaspoon salt*

Preheat oven to 375 degrees. Set out an ungreased 10-inch tube pan.

In a medium bowl, combine the flour and cocoa powder with ¾ cup of sugar. Sift these together three separate times. Set aside.

Place the egg whites in a standing mixer bowl and, using the whisk attachment, turn mixer to lowest speed. After 1 minute, add the cream of tartar, vanilla, and salt. After another minute of beating, turn the mixer to medium speed and gradually add the remaining ¾ cup sugar. Stop and scrape the sides of the bowl with a rubber spatula when all the sugar has been added. Resume beating until the whites are stiff but moist, about 3 to 5 minutes. Transfer the mixture to a large bowl.

Sift the flour-sugar mixture a fourth time over the egg white mixture and gently fold until all the dry ingredients are mixed in.

Fill the pan immediately and smooth the top with a rubber spatula. Bake for 30 to 40 minutes. Test for doneness at 30 minutes; if tester comes out clean with no traces of batter, it is done. The cake should be lightly browned and spring back when pressed gently with finger. Remove from the oven and allow to cool in the pan for 30 minutes. Remove from the pan and cool completely on a wire rack (place the pan upside down on an empty bottle for easier removal).

SERVES 10 TO 12.

Chocolate Cherry Upside-Down Cake

Preheat oven to 350 degrees.

Grease a 9 x 13-inch pan.

Spread the pie filling evenly over the bottom of prepared pan. Set aside.

In a large bowl, stir together the flour, sugar, cocoa powder, baking soda, and salt until completely combined. Set aside.

In a small bowl, combine the water, oil, vinegar, and vanilla. Add to the flour mixture and stir until just moistened. Pour the batter evenly over the pie filling, using a small spatula to smooth if needed.

Bake for 30 to 35 minutes, or until a cake tester inserted into the center of the cake comes out clean. Let cool for 10 minutes in the pan, then invert the pan onto a serving dish and continue to cool. Best if served warm.

SERVES 8 TO 10.

1 (21-ounce) can cherry pie filling

2¼ cups all-purpose flour

1½ cups sugar

¾ cup unsweetened cocoa powder

1½ teaspoons baking soda

¼ teaspoon salt

1½ cups water

½ cup vegetable oil

¼ cup distilled white vinegar

1 teaspoon vanilla extract

Mississippi Mud Cake

You'll be hard-pressed to find a more dense, fudgy, deeply decadent chocolate cake than this one. The ganache only makes it more stupendous.

CAKE INGREDIENTS:

2 to 3 tablespoons cocoa powder for dusting

2 cups all-purpose flour

1 teaspoon baking soda

¼ teaspoon salt

1¾ cups strong brewed coffee

¼ cup coffee liqueur (such as Kahlúa)

8 ounces unsweetened chocolate

1 cup (2 sticks) unsalted butter, softened

2 cups sugar

2 large eggs, lightly beaten

1 teaspoon vanilla extract

GANACHE

INGREDIENTS:

2 ounces semisweet chocolate

2 tablespoons heavy cream

Preheat oven to 275 degrees.

Butter a 10-inch Bundt or tube pan and lightly dust with cocoa powder.

In a medium bowl, sift the flour, baking soda, and salt. Set aside.

In a large saucepan, heat the coffee and liqueur on low heat for about 5 minutes. Add the chocolate and butter into the coffee mixture and stir until melted. When smooth, add the sugar and stir until dissolved. Let this mixture cool for 20 minutes.

When cool, transfer to a large bowl. On the medium speed of an electric mixer, add the flour mixture in thirds, blending well after each addition. Then add the eggs and vanilla. Beat for another minute or so.

Bake for 70 to 80 minutes, or until a cake tester inserted into the center of the cake comes out with moist crumbs attached. Cool in the pan for 10 minutes, then invert the cake and pan onto a plate, but do not remove the pan until the cake is completely cool.

To make the ganache: Place the chocolate and cream in a small saucepan and melt over low heat, stirring occasionally until smooth. Serve right away over completely cooled cake.

SERVES 12 TO 16.

Oma Rose's Marble Cake

Preheat oven to 350 degrees.

Grease and lightly flour a 10-inch tube pan.

In a medium bowl, add the vanilla extract to the egg whites and beat on high with an electric mixer until stiff peaks form. Set aside.

In a large bowl, cream the butter and sugar on the medium speed of an electric mixer until fluffy, about 3 minutes. Add the egg yolks and beat well. Next, add the flour and the milk, alternating in three parts, beating well after each addition. Stir in the lemon juice. Remove the bowl from the mixer and gently fold the egg whites into the mixture until no streaks of white are showing.

Remove one-third of the batter to another bowl. To this, add the cocoa powder and mix until the cocoa is completely incorporated.

Take the prepared pan and, alternating, add the two batters, starting with the white batter, then the cocoa batter, and again the white batter. Smooth each layer of batter with a spatula as you go. Make 5 layers of batter.

Bake for 50 to 60 minutes, or until a cake tester inserted into the center of the cake comes out clean. Let the cake cool in the pan for 15 minutes. Remove to a rack to cool completely. Sprinkle with powdered sugar before serving.

SERVES 12 TO 16.

1 tablespoon vanilla extract

6 large eggs, separated

1 cup (2 sticks) unsalted butter, softened

1 cup sugar

2⅔ cups self-rising flour

¾ cup milk

2 tablespoons lemon juice

5 tablespoons unsweetened cocoa powder

Confectioners' sugar to garnish

Teatime Hazelnut Apple Cake

This is a low-fat version of a favorite cake of mine. It's full of fresh fruit and fragrant toasted nuts.

1½ cups all-purpose flour

1½ cups whole-wheat flour

1 teaspoon baking soda

1 teaspoon baking powder

1 teaspoon ground cinnamon

¼ teaspoon ground cardamom

1½ cups vegetable oil

2 cups firmly packed light brown sugar

3 large egg whites

3 tablespoons apple juice

2 teaspoons vanilla extract

3 cups Golden Delicious apples, peeled, cored, and chopped (about 3 to 5 apples)

1 cup coarsely chopped hazelnuts

Confectioners' sugar to garnish

Preheat oven to 350 degrees.

Grease and flour a 10-inch tube pan.

In a medium bowl, sift the flours together with the baking soda, baking powder, and spices. Set aside.

In a large bowl, beat the oil and brown sugar on the medium speed of an electric mixer until creamy, about 1 minute. Add the egg whites, mixing thoroughly. Next, add the flour mixture in three parts to the egg mixture, mixing well until thoroughly combined. Add the apple juice and vanilla. Turn off the mixer and fold in the apple and nuts until thoroughly combined.

Pour the batter into the prepared pan, and bake for 45 to 55 minutes, or until a cake tester inserted into the center of the cake comes out clean. Let the cake cool in the pan for 10 minutes, then remove to a rack to cool completely. Sprinkle with powdered sugar before serving.

SERVES 12 TO 16.

Your Not-So-Basic Pound Cake

> *I have a great fondness for pound cake; I love to be able to dress it up or down with sauces, whipped cream, syrup, whatever strikes my fancy. Here's a truly delicious and mouthwatering pound cake with a few variations to change it around if you like.*

4 cups all-purpose flour

2 teaspoons baking powder

2 cups (4 sticks) unsalted butter, softened

3 cups sugar

6 large eggs, at room temperature

½ cup milk

½ cup sour cream

2 teaspoons vanilla extract

2 tablespoons finely grated lemon zest

Confectioners' sugar for garnish

Preheat oven to 350 degrees.

Grease and flour a 10-inch Bundt pan.

In a medium bowl, combine the flour and the baking powder. Set aside.

In a large bowl, cream the butter on the medium speed of an electric mixer until smooth, about 1 minute. Then add in the sugar and beat for 3 minutes or so, until fluffy. Add the eggs one at a time, until well incorporated. Add in half the flour mixture, alternating with the milk, until well blended. Add the other half of the dry ingredients, alternating with the sour cream. Stir in the vanilla and lemon zest until thoroughly mixed.

Pour the batter into the prepared pan and bake for 60 to 70 minutes, or until a cake tester inserted into the center of the cake comes out clean. Let the cake cool in the pan, then remove to a rack to cool completely. Sprinkle with powdered sugar before serving.

SERVES 12 TO 16.

★ VARIATIONS ★

Butterscotch Pecan Pound Cake

Replace the white sugar with dark brown sugar, and add 2 cups of coarsely chopped pecans to the batter.

Tennessee Whiskey Pound Cake

Make the pound cake recipe above, replacing the milk with whiskey.

Cheesecakes

Coffee lovers will love the subtle, rich taste of this cheesecake.

Cappuccino Cheesecake

Preheat oven to 325 degrees.

Grease the bottom of a 9-inch springform pan.

To make the crust: In a small bowl, combine the butter with the crumbs, sugar, and espresso powder. Press into the bottom of the prepared pan. Bake for 10 minutes. Remove from the oven and cool on a rack.

To make the filling: In a large bowl, beat the cream cheese on the low speed of an electric mixer until smooth. Gradually add the sugar. Add the eggs one at a time. Stop the mixer and scrape down the sides and bottom of the bowl with a rubber spatula. Mix in the flour until just blended. Stir in the sour cream, mixing thoroughly. Then stir in the espresso powder and cinnamon.

Pour the batter into the prepared pan, and wrap the bottom of the pan with aluminum foil. Set the pan in a one-inch water bath. Bake until the edges are set and the center moves only slightly when the pan is shaken, about 50 to 60 minutes.

Turn off the heat and keep the oven door slightly open while cooling the cake in the oven for about 1 hour before removing. Cover and refrigerate for at least 6 to 8 hours.

Remove the cheesecake from the refrigerator at least 15 to 30 minutes before serving.

MAKES 10 TO 12 SERVINGS.

CRUST INGREDIENTS:

1/4 cup (1/2 stick) unsalted butter, melted

1 1/2 cups chocolate cookie crumbs

2 tablespoons sugar

2 teaspoons instant espresso powder

FILLING INGREDIENTS:

2 (8-ounce) packages cream cheese, softened

1 cup sugar

4 large eggs, at room temperature

3 tablespoons all-purpose flour

1 cup sour cream

2 tablespoons instant espresso powder

1/8 teaspoon ground cinnamon

Cherry-Topped Macaroon Cheescake

Many people adore a New York–style cheesecake. I like mine with this slight variation on the usual graham cracker crust, slathered with sweet cherries.

CRUST INGREDIENTS:

¼ cup (½ stick) unsalted butter, melted

1½ cups coconut macaroon cookie crumbs

¼ teaspoon ground cinnamon

FILLING INGREDIENTS:

2 (8-ounce) packages cream cheese, softened

1 cup sugar

3 large eggs, at room temperature

1 teaspoon vanilla extract

1 tablespoon finely grated lemon zest

2 cups sour cream

GARNISH:

1 (21-ounce) can cherry pie filling

Preheat oven to 325 degrees.

Grease the bottom of a 9-inch springform pan.

To make the crust: In a small bowl, combine the butter with the crumbs and cinnamon. Press into the bottom of the prepared pan. Bake for 10 minutes. Remove from the oven and cool on a rack.

To make the filling: In a large bowl, beat the cream cheese on the low speed of an electric mixer until very smooth. Gradually add the sugar. Add the eggs one at a time. Stop the mixer and scrape down the sides of the bowl with a rubber spatula. Stir in the vanilla and zest until well combined. Then stir in the sour cream, mixing thoroughly.

Pour the batter into the prepared pan, and wrap the bottom of the pan with aluminum foil. Set the pan in a one-inch water bath. Bake until the edges are set and the center moves only slightly when the pan is shaken, about 50 to 60 minutes.

Turn off the heat and keep the oven door slightly open while cooling the cake in the oven for about 1 hour before removing. Cover and refrigerate for at least 6 to 8 hours.

Remove the cheesecake from the refrigerator at least 15 to 30 minutes before serving. Garnish the cheesecake with cherries just before serving.

MAKES 10 TO 12 SERVINGS.

Lime Cheesecake with Gingersnap Crust

> While Key limes are sometimes hard to find, their flavor imparts a special liveliness to this confection. Bottled Key lime juice is fairly available; feel free to use regular limes if need be, although your cheesecake will be slightly less tangy.

Preheat oven to 325 degrees.

Grease the bottom of a 9-inch springform pan.

To make the crust: In a small bowl, combine the butter with the crumbs and sugar. Press into the bottom of the prepared pan. Bake for 10 minutes. Remove from the oven and cool on a rack.

To make the filling: In a large bowl, beat the cream cheese on the low speed of an electric mixer until very smooth. Gradually add the sugar. Add the eggs one at a time. Stop the mixer and scrape down the sides of the bowl with a rubber spatula. Stir in the lime juice and zest until well combined. Then stir in the sour cream, mixing thoroughly.

Pour the batter into the prepared pan, and wrap the bottom of the pan with aluminum foil. Set the pan in a one-inch water bath. Bake until the edges are set and the center moves only slightly when the pan is shaken, about 50 to 60 minutes.

Turn off the heat, and keep the oven door slightly open while cooling the cake in the oven for about 1 hour before removing. Cover and refrigerate for at least 6 to 8 hours.

Remove the cheesecake from the refrigerator at least 15 to 30 minutes before serving. Garnish the cheesecake with fresh lime slices just before serving.

MAKES 10 TO 12 SERVINGS.

CRUST INGREDIENTS:
1/4 cup (1/2 stick) unsalted butter, melted
1 1/2 cups gingersnap cookie crumbs
2 tablespoons sugar

FILLING INGREDIENTS:
3 (8-ounce) packages cream cheese, softened
1 cup sugar
3 large eggs, at room temperature
2/3 cup fresh lime juice (or Key lime juice)
1 tablespoon finely grated lime zest
1/2 cup sour cream

GARNISH:
Fresh lime slices

Low-fat White Chocolate Raspberry Cheesecake

My taste testers for this cheesecake couldn't believe this was a completely low-fat, lower-sugar recipe. Try it for yourself and be pleasantly surprised by the results.

CRUST INGREDIENTS:

¼ cup (½ stick) unsalted butter, melted

1½ cups chocolate wafer crumbs

FILLING INGREDIENTS:

1 (10-ounce) package frozen unsweetened raspberries, thawed, pureed, and strained

1 tablespoon raspberry liqueur

1 teaspoon cornstarch

6 ounces white chocolate, coarsely chopped

3 (8-ounce) packages low-fat cream cheese, softened

¼ cup Splenda Sugar Blend for Baking

¾ cup egg substitute (or amount equivalent to 3 large eggs)

Preheat oven to 325 degrees.

Grease the bottom of a 9-inch springform pan.

To make the crust: In a small bowl, combine the butter with the crumbs. Press into the bottom of the prepared pan. Bake for 10 minutes. Remove from the oven and cool on a rack.

In a small saucepan, combine the pureed raspberries, liqueur, and cornstarch, stirring well. Cook and stir over medium heat until thickened and bubbly. Cook and stir 2 minutes more. Set aside to cool. Meanwhile, in a double boiler over just-simmering water, melt the chocolate over low heat, stirring frequently. Set this aside to cool also.

To make the filling: In a large bowl, beat the cream cheese on the low speed of an electric mixer until smooth. Gradually add the Splenda. Add the egg substitute and blend. Stop the mixer and scrape down the sides and bottom of the bowl with a rubber spatula. Mix in the cooled chocolate until well blended.

Pour the batter into the prepared pan. Spoon about ½ cup of the raspberry mixture over the filling. Using the tip of a sharp knife, swirl the mixture into the batter, forming a decorative marbleized pattern. (Cover and chill the remaining raspberry sauce; return to room temperature before serving.) Wrap the bottom of the pan with aluminum foil, and set the pan in a one-inch water bath. Bake until the edges are set and the center moves only slightly when the pan is shaken, about 50 to 60 minutes.

Turn off the heat, and keep the oven door slightly open while cooling the cake in the oven for about 1 hour before removing. Cover and refrigerate for at least 6 to 8 hours.

Remove the cheesecake from the refrigerator at least 15 to 30 minutes before serving. Spoon the reserved raspberry sauce over each slice if desired.

MAKES 10 TO 12 SERVINGS.

Peanut Butter Cheesecake

> *Drizzle your favorite jelly over this cheesecake after it's cool to make a luscious "PB and J" cheesecake.*

CRUST INGREDIENTS:

¼ cup (½ stick) unsalted butter, melted

1¼ cups graham cracker crumbs

3 tablespoons light brown sugar

¼ cup finely chopped peanuts

FILLING INGREDIENTS:

2 (8-ounce) packages cream cheese, softened

¾ cup chunky peanut butter

1 cup sugar

4 large eggs, at room temperature

2 tablespoons all-purpose flour

½ cup milk

Preheat oven to 325 degrees.

Grease the bottom of a 9-inch springform pan.

To make the crust: In a small bowl, combine the butter with the crumbs, brown sugar, and peanuts. Press into the bottom of the prepared pan. Bake for 10 minutes. Remove from the oven and cool on a rack.

To make the filling: In a large bowl, beat the cream cheese and peanut butter on the low speed of an electric mixer until very smooth. Gradually add the sugar. Add the eggs one at a time. Stop the mixer and scrape down the sides and bottom of the bowl with a rubber spatula. Mix in the flour until just blended. Then stir in the milk, mixing thoroughly.

Pour the batter into the prepared pan, and wrap the bottom of the pan with aluminum foil. Set the pan in a one-inch water bath. Bake until the edges are set and the center moves only slightly when the pan is shaken, about 50 to 60 minutes.

Turn off the heat, and keep the oven door slightly open while cooling the cake in the oven for about 1 hour before removing. Cover and refrigerate for at least 6 to 8 hours.

Remove the cheesecake from the refrigerator at least 15 to 30 minutes before serving.

MAKES 10 TO 12 SERVINGS.

Pumpkin Bourbon Cheesecake

A seemingly perfect fall dessert, this is wonderful to serve with Thanksgiving dinner in addition to or as an alternative to pumpkin pie.

Preheat oven to 325 degrees.

Grease the bottom of a 9-inch springform pan.

To make the crust: In a small bowl, combine the butter with the crumbs, brown sugar, and pecans. Press into the bottom of the prepared pan. Bake for 10 minutes. Remove from the oven and cool on a rack.

To make the filling: In a large bowl, beat the cream cheese and pumpkin puree on the low speed of an electric mixer until very smooth. Gradually add the sugars. Add the eggs one at a time, then blend in the spices. Stop the mixer and scrape down the sides of the bowl with a rubber spatula. Stir in the heavy cream, vanilla, and bourbon, mixing thoroughly.

Pour the batter into the prepared pan, and wrap the bottom of the pan with aluminum foil. Set the pan in a one-inch water bath. Bake until the edges are set and the center moves only slightly when the pan is shaken, about 50 to 60 minutes.

Turn off the heat, and keep the oven door slightly open while cooling the cake in the oven for about 1 hour before removing. Cover and refrigerate for at least 6 to 8 hours.

Remove the cheesecake from the refrigerator at least 15 to 30 minutes before serving.

To make the topping: In a medium bowl, whip the heavy cream on the high speed of an electric mixer until soft peaks form. Add the bourbon, if desired. Smooth over top of cheesecake just before serving, and sprinkle decoratively with chopped pecans.

MAKES 10 TO 12 SERVINGS.

CRUST INGREDIENTS:
5 tablespoons unsalted butter, softened
1 cup graham cracker crumbs
¼ cup light brown sugar
¾ cup finely chopped pecans

FILLING INGREDIENTS:
3 (8-ounce) packages cream cheese, softened
1 cup pumpkin puree
½ cup sugar
½ cup firmly packed light brown sugar
3 large eggs, at room temperature
2 teaspoons ground cinnamon
½ teaspoon ground ginger
2 tablespoons heavy cream
1 teaspoon vanilla extract
1½ tablespoons bourbon whiskey

TOPPING INGREDIENTS:
1 cup heavy cream
1 tablespoon bourbon whiskey (optional)
Chopped pecans to garnish

Pies and Tarts, Crisps and Cobblers

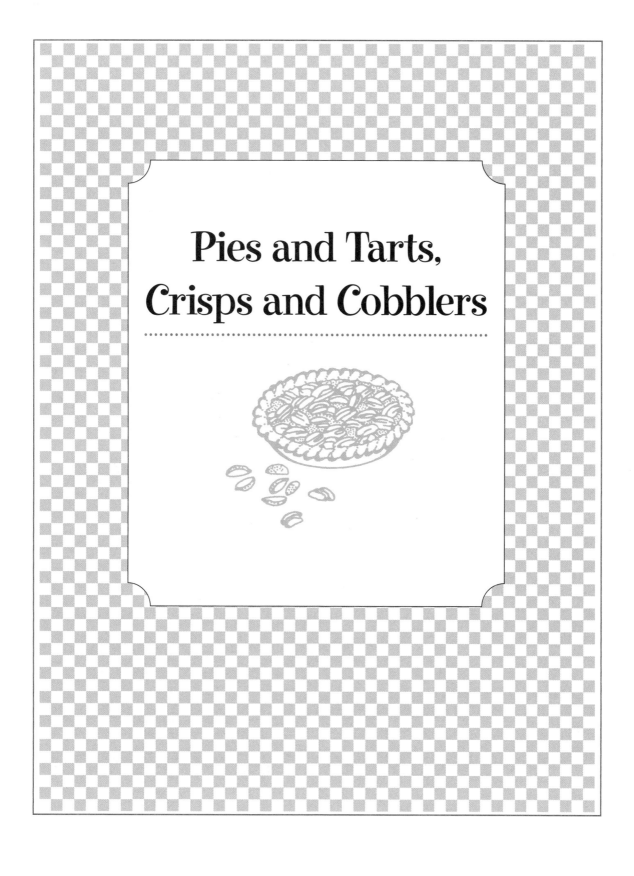

Apple Strawberry Double-Crust Pie

> With seasonal fruit readily available all year, why not mix the best of summer and fall in a pie? I particularly love this combination, and while I also love crumb toppings, I think the double crust adds that just-right homey touch to this pie.

Preheat oven to 425 degrees.

To make the crust: Place the flour, sugar, and salt in a large bowl and, using a pastry blender, cut in the butter until the mixture resembles coarse cornmeal. Sprinkle the ice water by tablespoons over the flour mixture, tossing with a fork until all of the dough is moistened. Form dough into a ball.

On a lightly floured surface, roll out half the dough to fit into a 9-inch glass pie dish. Fold the edges under all around the rim and crimp. Roll out the remaining dough and set it aside on a piece of wax paper or lightly floured surface.

To make the filling: In a large bowl, combine the sugars and cornstarch and whisk to combine. Stir in the fruit and gently toss until coated. Transfer this into the pie crust and dot with slices of butter. Moisten the edges of the bottom crust and place the other crust directly on top, pressing the top crust down at the edges. Trim the top pastry with a knife, and press the edges together with the tines of a fork. With a sharp knife, cut a small *X* in the center of the top crust to allow steam to escape during baking.

Bake for 25 minutes, until juices are bubbling and the crust has begun to brown. Reduce the heat to 350 degrees and bake for another 20 to 25 minutes, until the top is well browned. Remove from the oven and let the pie cool on a rack for at least 30 minutes before serving.

SERVES 6 TO 8.

DOUBLE CRUST INGREDIENTS:

3 cups all-purpose flour

2 tablespoons sugar

$\frac{1}{2}$ teaspoon salt

1 cup (2 sticks) cold unsalted butter, cut into small pieces ·

4 to 5 tablespoons ice water (a bit more if needed)

FILLING INGREDIENTS:

$\frac{1}{3}$ cup sugar

$\frac{1}{3}$ cup firmly packed light brown sugar

3 tablespoons cornstarch

1 pint cleaned, hulled, sliced strawberries

2 small apples, peeled, cored, and chopped

1 to 2 tablespoons cold unsalted butter

Blueberry Cobbler

> *I'm a sucker for warm, fruity confections; besides ice cream, they're my idea of a perfect dessert. This American classic never fails to please, and the addition of ginger and almond enhances the flavors in just the right way.*

FILLING INGREDIENTS:

3 cups fresh or frozen blueberries, rinsed and drained

1/4 cup sugar

1 tablespoon cornstarch

1/8 teaspoon ground ginger

1 1/2 teaspoons almond extract

TOPPING INGREDIENTS:

1 cup all-purpose flour

1 1/2 teaspoons baking powder

2 tablespoons sugar

1/4 teaspoon salt

1/4 cup (1/2 stick) unsalted butter, chilled

3 to 4 tablespoons milk

1 to 2 tablespoons sugar for sprinkling

Preheat oven to 400 degrees.

To make the filling: In a medium bowl, toss the berries, sugar, cornstarch, ginger, and almond extract, coating the berries evenly. Set this aside in a 2-quart casserole dish.

To make the topping: In another bowl, sift the flour, baking powder, sugar, and salt. Add the butter, one tablespoon at a time, and work the mixture with your fingers until pea-sized crumbs are formed. Gradually add the milk until a sticky dough is formed. Knead the dough on a lightly floured surface a few times until it is smooth. Spread the dough by lightly stretching it on top of the berries. Sprinkle the top evenly with sugar and bake for 25 to 35 minutes, or until the biscuit topping is golden and the fruit is bubbly. Serve warm.

SERVES 6 TO 8.

Bourbon Pecan Pie

Preheat oven to 375 degrees.

To make the crust: Place the flour, sugar, and salt in a large bowl and, using a pastry blender, cut in the butter until the mixture resembles coarse cornmeal. Sprinkle the ice water by tablespoons over the flour mixture, tossing with a fork until all of the dough is moistened. Form dough into a ball. On a lightly floured surface, roll out the dough to fit into a 9-inch glass pie dish. Fold the edges under all around the rim and crimp.

To make the filling: In a medium bowl, beat the eggs with a whisk. Add in the remaining ingredients (except for the pecans) in the order listed, stirring until just mixed. Place the pecans in the bottom of the pastry shell and pour the mixture over them. Bake for 35 to 40 minutes, or until the edges of the pie are set and the center quivers slightly when shaken.

Allow to cool completely before serving. Serve with a scoop of vanilla ice cream if desired.

SERVES 6 TO 8.

CRUST INGREDIENTS:

1½ cups all-purpose flour

1 tablespoon sugar

¼ teaspoon salt

½ cup (1 stick) cold unsalted butter, cut into small pieces

2 to 3 tablespoons ice water

FILLING INGREDIENTS:

3 large eggs, at room temperature

1 cup sugar

½ cup light corn syrup

½ cup dark corn syrup

⅓ cup (5⅓ tablespoons) unsalted butter, melted

3 tablespoons bourbon whiskey

¼ teaspoon salt

1 cup coarsely chopped pecans

Chess Pie

One of several very old American pie recipes, this classic is rarely seen in cookbooks nowadays. It takes only a few minutes of assembly to produce this vintage creamy custard pie.

CRUST INGREDIENTS:

1½ cups all-purpose flour

1 tablespoon sugar

¼ teaspoon salt

½ cup (1 stick) cold unsalted butter, cut into small pieces

2 to 3 tablespoons ice water

FILLING INGREDIENTS:

½ cup (1 stick) unsalted butter

½ cup firmly packed light brown sugar

1 cup sugar

3 large eggs, lightly beaten

1 tablespoon distilled white vinegar

2 teaspoons vanilla extract

1 tablespoon cornmeal

Preheat oven to 400 degrees.

To make the crust: Place the flour, sugar, and salt in a large bowl and, using a pastry blender, cut in the butter until the mixture resembles coarse cornmeal. Sprinkle the ice water by tablespoons over the flour mixture, tossing with a fork until all of the dough is moistened. Form dough into a ball. On a lightly floured surface, roll out the dough to fit into a 9-inch glass pie dish. Fold the edges under all around the rim and crimp.

To make the filling: Melt the butter and sugars in a medium saucepan on a medium flame, stirring constantly. Remove from the heat and cool slightly. Add the remaining ingredients, in the order listed, and stir (but do not beat) until well mixed.

Pour the filling into the prepared pie shell and bake at 400 degrees for 15 minutes. Reduce the heat to 350 degrees and bake for another 20 to 30 minutes. The pie is done when the center quivers slightly when shaken.

Cool completely before serving, and refrigerate leftovers.

SERVES 6 TO 8.

My mother should be world famous for this recipe alone! This is one of the best desserts I have ever eaten, hands down (again, my weakness for fruity comfort desserts comes through). While Italian prune plums are best for this tart, they are not always available. If using slightly larger plums, make sure to cut them into smaller pieces, such as sixths or even eighths.

Lay out a 9 x 13-inch baking sheet.

In a medium bowl, combine the flour, sugar, and baking powder. Add in the butter, several tablespoons at a time, and begin to knead, forming crumbs. Then add the egg mixture until the dough comes together. Work the dough several times on a floured surface. Roll into a ball, wrap in plastic wrap, and refrigerate for at least 2 hours, or overnight.

Preheat oven to 350 degrees.

Allow the dough to come to room temperature. Flour a board, and roll out the dough into a rectangle about $\frac{1}{4}$ inch thick. Place it onto the baking sheet, and gently stretch the dough out to the corners, making sure not to break the dough. Smooth the surface with a large piece of wax paper. Prick the dough lightly all over the surface with a fork.

Arrange the halved plums (fleshy side up) close together on the dough, leaving about $\frac{1}{2}$ inch all around as a border (the plums should just be touching each other). Sprinkle the plums with a few tablespoons of sugar. Bake for 25 to 35 minutes at 350 degrees, until the plums are cooked and a bit brown in color, and the edges of the dough are lightly golden.

Allow to cool for 30 minutes or so before cutting and serving. Serve with whipped cream if desired.

SERVES 8 TO 10.

2 cups all-purpose flour

5 tablespoons sugar, plus more for sprinkling

$\frac{1}{8}$ teaspoon baking powder

7 tablespoons cold unsalted butter, cut into small pieces

1 egg, mixed with 1 teaspoon water and $\frac{1}{2}$ teaspoon vanilla

2 to $2\frac{1}{2}$ pounds ripe small plums, pitted and sliced in half

Peach Pandowdy

While a pandowdy differs very little from a cobbler (the addition of the egg gives a cakey topping versus a biscuit topping), this ultimate comfort food is a mouthwatering treat.

FILLING INGREDIENTS:

4 cups (4 to 6 medium) fresh peaches, peeled, pitted, and sliced

¼ cup sugar

¼ cupcup water

½ teaspoon ground nutmeg

⅛ teaspoon ground cloves

1 tablespoon cornstarch

TOPPING

INGREDIENTS:

1 cup all-purpose flour

2 tablespoons sugar

1½ teaspoons baking powder

¼ teaspoon salt

¼ cup (½ stick) unsalted butter, chilled

1 large egg, lightly beaten

3 to 4 tablespoons milk

2 tablespoons sugar, mixed with ⅛ teaspoon cinnamon for sprinkling

Preheat oven to 400 degrees.

Place peaches in an 8 x 8-inch baking pan. In a medium saucepan, combine the sugar, water, spices, and cornstarch; mix well. Bring to a boil and boil for 1 minute. Pour the syrup over the peaches.

In a medium bowl, stir together the flour, sugar, baking powder, and salt. Cut in the butter, and mix with your fingers until crumbly. Stir in the egg, and then the milk, one tablespoon at a time, to make a moist but not too sticky dough. Knead the dough on a lightly floured surface a few times until it is smooth. Place the dough over the peaches; sprinkle with cinnamon sugar.

Bake 25 to 35 minutes, or until golden brown and bubbly around the edges.

Serve warm, with a scoop of vanilla ice cream if desired.

SERVES 6 TO 8.

Pear Nectarine Crisp

Preheat oven to 350 degrees.

To prepare the crisp: In a large bowl, toss the pears and the nectarines with the water, sugar, cornstarch, and spices. Arrange the fruit in the bottom of a greased 8-inch deep-dish baking pan. Set aside.

To prepare the topping: In a medium bowl, mix together the flour, sugar, oats, and pecans. Using a pastry blender, cut in the butter until the mixture resembles coarse crumbs. Sprinkle evenly over the fruit and bake for 40 to 45 minutes, or until the juices are bubbling and the crumbs are lightly golden. Serve warm with whipped cream if desired.

SERVES 6 TO 8.

CRISP INGREDIENTS:

2 cups peeled, cored, and sliced pears (about 2 medium Bosc pears)

2 cups peeled, pitted, sliced nectarines (about 2 to 3 medium nectarines)

$1/4$ cup water

3 tablespoons sugar

1 tablespoon cornstarch

$1/2$ teaspoon ground cinnamon

$1/8$ teaspoon ground ginger

TOPPING INGREDIENTS:

1 cup all-purpose flour

$2/3$ cup light brown sugar

$1/2$ cup rolled oats (not quick-cooking oats)

3 tablespoons finely chopped pecans

10 tablespoons unsalted butter, softened

Sour Cream Raisin Pie

This is also known as old-fashioned vinegar pie, another classic recipe dating back to the nineteenth century. I like to bake this on a lower temperature than most pies (instead of starting the oven high and turning the temperature down) because of the delicate nature of the filling.

CRUST INGREDIENTS:

1½ cups all-purpose flour

1 tablespoon sugar

¼ teaspoon salt

½ cup (1 stick) cold unsalted butter, cut into small pieces

2 to 3 tablespoons ice water

FILLING INGREDIENTS:

5 large eggs, at room temperature

2 cups all-purpose flour

1 cup sugar

3 tablespoons unsalted butter, melted

3 tablespoons apple cider vinegar

1 teaspoon vanilla extract

½ cup raisins (dark or golden)

½ teaspoon ground cinnamon

¼ teaspoon ground nutmeg

¼ teaspoon ground cloves

1 cup sour cream

Preheat oven to 300 degrees.

To make the crust: Place the flour, sugar, and salt in a large bowl and, using a pastry blender, cut in the butter until the mixture resembles coarse cornmeal.

Sprinkle the ice water by tablespoons over the flour mixture, tossing with a fork until all of the dough is moistened. Form dough into a ball. On a lightly floured surface, roll out the dough to fit into a 9-inch glass pie dish. Fold the edges under all around the rim and crimp.

To make the filling: In a large bowl, first beat the eggs with a whisk. Add in the remaining ingredients in the order listed, stirring until just mixed.

Pour the filling into the prepared crust and bake for 60 minutes, or until the edges of the pie are set and the center quivers slightly when shaken.

You can serve this pie warm or cold.

SERVES 6 TO 8.

Puddings and
Icebox Desserts

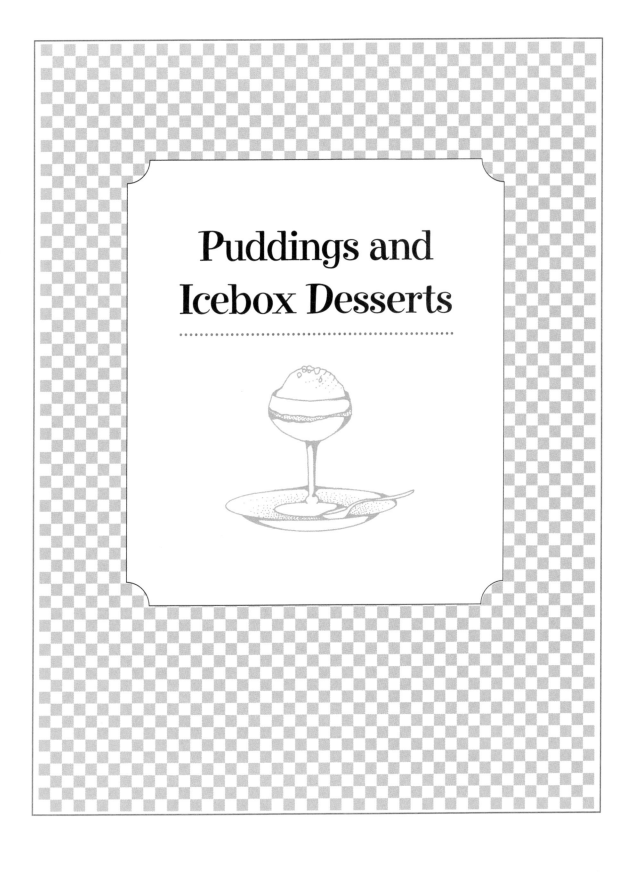

Fans of butterscotch will agree that this creamy, dreamy, satiny pudding is heavenly. If you're like me, you might want to make two recipes' worth if you're expecting company, since you'll likely eat one batch by yourself.

Butterscotch Pudding

In a heavy-bottomed saucepan, combine the butter, brown sugar, and salt. Cook over low heat, whisking until the sugar has dissolved.

In a small bowl, mix together the cornstarch with $\frac{1}{2}$ cup of the half-and-half until the cornstarch is dissolved. Set aside.

Add $\frac{1}{2}$ cup of plain half-and-half to the saucepan, whisking until incorporated. Add the remaining 1 cup of half-and-half, and then the cornstarch mixture and stir to combine. Increase the heat to medium-high and cook, whisking constantly, until thickened, about 3 to 4 minutes. Remove from the heat and stir in the whiskey and vanilla.

Spoon the pudding into dessert cups and refrigerate at least 2 hours. Cover each one with plastic if you don't want a skin forming on the top. Garnish with whipped cream if desired.

SERVES 4.

3 tablespoons unsalted butter

$\frac{1}{2}$ cup plus 2 tablespoons firmly packed dark brown sugar

$\frac{1}{4}$ teaspoon salt

3 tablespoons cornstarch

2 cups half-and-half, divided

2 tablespoons whiskey

$\frac{1}{2}$ teaspoon vanilla extract

Chocolate Chiffon Dessert Cups

This oh-so-simple dessert is best made using a food processor to ensure a smooth, mousselike product. You'll hardly believe it is made with ricotta cheese.

3 ounces unsweetened chocolate, melted

1 (15-ounce) container ricotta cheese, whole milk or part-skim

1 teaspoon vanilla extract

2/3 cup superfine sugar (to taste)

1 to 2 tablespoons milk

GARNISH:
Whipped cream or dessert topping
Fresh raspberries
Chocolate chips

In a food processor, blend the chocolate, ricotta cheese, and vanilla until very smooth. Add the sugar gradually until well incorporated, and then gradually add the milk. Pour into dessert cups and chill.

Before serving, top with whipped cream, fresh berries, or chocolate chips if desired.

SERVES 6.

Chocolate Sandwich Cookie Bread Pudding

With a great fondness for bread pudding, my husband asked me to try one with his favorite cookies baked right in. What a great suggestion!

Preheat oven to 350 degrees.

Lightly grease a 2-quart baking dish, then place the bread crumbs and cookies inside. Set aside.

In a medium bowl, blend the remaining ingredients until thoroughly combined. Pour over the bread mixture, stirring to coat evenly. Bake for 45 to 50 minutes, or until a cake tester inserted into center of the pudding comes out clean, and the top is bubbly.

Serve warm or at room temperature, topped with whipped cream if desired.

SERVES 6 TO 8.

4 cups coarse bread crumbs (coarsely cut day-old French bread will do)

16 chocolate sandwich cookies, coarsely broken

2 cups milk

$\frac{1}{2}$ cup sugar

$\frac{1}{4}$ cup ($\frac{1}{2}$ stick) unsalted butter, melted

2 large eggs, lightly beaten

$\frac{1}{4}$ teaspoon salt

1 teaspoon vanilla extract

Lemon Magic Pudding

> *You'll be amazed that this simple batter magically produces both a light sponge cake and delicious, creamy pudding.*

3 large eggs, separated

$\frac{1}{2}$ cup sugar

$\frac{1}{3}$ cup all-purpose flour

$\frac{1}{4}$ teaspoon salt

2 teaspoons finely grated lemon zest

$\frac{1}{4}$ cup lemon juice

1 tablespoon unsalted butter, melted

$\frac{3}{4}$ cup milk

Preheat oven to 350 degrees.

Lightly grease a 2-quart baking dish.

In a medium bowl, on the medium-high speed of an electric mixer, beat the egg whites until stiff but not dry.

In another bowl, combine the sugar, flour, and salt. Whisk in the zest, lemon juice, butter, milk, and egg yolks. Gently fold the beaten whites into this mixture until no streaks of white are showing.

Pour the mixture into the prepared dish. Place the dish in a water bath (a cookie sheet with high sides, or a large baking pan) of about one inch of water. Bake for 35 to 40 minutes, or until top is lightly golden.

Serve this dish warm or cold.

MAKES 4 TO 6 SERVINGS.

Low-fat Chocolate Raspberry Bread Pudding with Raspberry Sauce

This amazing recipe works just as well with whole milk and eggs, or low-fat milk and egg whites only. I generally make this pudding with 1 percent milk and use two egg whites and two whole eggs. You can mix and match to increase and decrease the fat content without sacrificing flavor.

For the pudding: Cut the French bread into 1-inch cubes and place in a 2-quart casserole dish. In a large bowl, combine the milk, cocoa powder, sugar, vanilla, and liqueur and whisk until well blended. Next, add the egg whites and stir. Pour the mixture over the bread. Cover with plastic wrap and place in the refrigerator for 45 minutes to 1 hour.

Preheat oven to 350 degrees.

Remove the plastic and bake for 45 minutes, until the top is slightly bubbly.

To make the sauce, puree the raspberries in a blender. Strain them through a sieve in order to remove the seeds. Add the sugar and stir until well blended. You can also leave some of the raspberries whole, and blend the rest, making a sauce that is a combination of whole and blended berries.

Allow the pudding to cool a bit. Serve warm with about 2 to 3 tablespoons of sauce poured over the top of each serving.

SERVES 8 TO 10.

PUDDING

INGREDIENTS:

1 standard-size loaf coarsely cut day-old French bread

4 cups low-fat milk

4 tablespoons unsweetened cocoa powder

¾ cup sugar

1 tablespoon vanilla extract

3 tablespoons raspberry liqueur (such as Chambord)

4 large egg whites

SAUCE INGREDIENTS:

1 (16-ounce) package frozen raspberries (not in syrup), thawed

3 tablespoons sugar

Mixed Berry Trifle

While these gorgeous trifle desserts are still considered somewhat English, they have made their way to the American dessert table with their elegant good looks, not to mention stunning taste. Feel free to experiment; mix the berries, or omit the liquor and add juice instead. To cut down on assembly time, use prepackaged cake and pudding mixes. The prettiest display is to use a footed trifle bowl, 8 inches wide. I prefer less cake and more fruit, so feel free to purchase another cake and layer it into the trifle.

2 (16-ounce) bags frozen unsweetened mixed berries, thawed

$\frac{1}{4}$ cup sugar (or more to taste)

1 tablespoon cornstarch

$\frac{1}{3}$ cup raspberry liqueur or sweet sherry

2 (3.4-ounce) packages instant vanilla pudding and pie mix

4 cups cold milk

1 teaspoon vanilla extract

1 (or 2) store-bought pound cake (12-ounce loaf)

1 cup heavy cream

A few tablespoons fresh raspberries

Place the thawed berries in a large sieve and drain over a bowl, making sure to reserve the drained syrup. Place the berries in a separate bowl and toss with sugar; set aside. Measure out 1 cup of the reserved syrup; if necessary, add enough water to bring up to 1 cup. Transfer $\frac{1}{4}$ cup of the syrup to a small saucepan. Add the cornstarch and stir to mix well. Stir in the remaining $\frac{3}{4}$ cup syrup. Bring this to a boil over medium-high heat, stirring occasionally. Lower the heat and stir in the liquor, cooking for another minute or so. Remove from the heat and pour over the fruit.

Make the pudding using the milk and vanilla extract (follow instructions on the box). Refrigerate until set.

Measure out and reserve $\frac{1}{2}$ cup of the fruit for garnish. Cut the cake into bite-size pieces using a serrated knife. Place half of the pieces into the trifle bowl. Spoon half the fruit over the cake; then cover with half of the pudding. Repeat, making 2 or 3 layers, using all the cake, fruit, and pudding.

Whip the heavy cream until stiff peaks form. Spread over the pudding until smooth. Garnish the top with the reserved fruit and fresh berries. Cover and refrigerate for at least 2 hours and up to 6 hours before serving.

SERVES 6 TO 10.

Baking with Kids

Candy Bar Ice Cream Pie

Beat the milk, pudding mixes, and half of the whipped topping in a medium bowl with a whisk for 1 minute (mixture will be somewhat thick).

Reserve ¼ cup of the cut-up candy bars. Stir the remaining candy into the pudding mixture. Set aside.

Layer half of the ice cream and then half the pudding mixture into the pie crust. Repeat layers. Spread the remaining whipped topping over the pudding layer in the crust. Sprinkle the top with the remaining candy. Cover with plastic wrap and freeze until the pie is firm, at least 30 minutes.

Let stand at room temperature 5 minutes before serving.

SERVES 6 TO 8.

1¼ cups cold milk

2 (3.9-ounce) packages chocolate or vanilla flavor instant pudding and pie filling

1 (8-ounce) container frozen nondairy whipped topping, thawed, divided

4 regular-size candy bars, such as Milky Way, Snickers, etc., cut into ¼-inch pieces, divided

1 quart vanilla ice cream

1 store-bought 9-inch chocolate pie crust

Cinnamon Yum-Yums

The smell of yeasty cinnamon buns wafting through the house is enough to get anybody up early. This is not the traditional yeast recipe, but a simpler version that tastes just as good. Kids will love kneading the dough and even younger kids can mix some ingredients.

DOUGH:

1¼ cups all-purpose flour

2 teaspoons baking powder

2 tablespoons sugar

¼ cup (½ stick) cold unsalted butter, cut into small pieces

1 large egg, at room temperature

¼ cup milk

FILLING:

3 tablespoons light brown sugar

2 teaspoons cinnamon

1 tablespoon unsalted butter, melted

ICING:

½ cup confectioners' sugar

1 teaspoon milk

Preheat oven to 375 degrees.

To make the dough: In a large bowl, sift the flour, baking powder, and sugar. Add the butter and rub the mixture between your fingertips until it looks crumbly like coarse cornmeal.

In a small bowl, mix together the egg and milk and whisk lightly. Add this to the flour mixture, stirring until just combined.

Turn the mixture onto a floured surface and gently knead 3 or 4 times, until it forms a dough. It will be slightly sticky, but do not add too much flour. Roll the dough out to roughly a 10-inch square.

In a small bowl, combine the brown sugar and cinnamon to make the filling. Brush the dough with the melted butter and sprinkle with the cinnamon-sugar mix. Fold the dough over, rolling it into a neat log about 10 inches across, and cut crosswise into 8 pieces.

Arrange the rolls on a baking sheet, flat side up, allowing the sides to touch. Press down to flatten the rolls a little. Bake in the oven for 15 to 18 minutes until golden and cooked through.

Prepare the icing by mixing the confectioners' sugar and milk in a small bowl until smooth. Drizzle over the warm buns.

MAKES 8 BUNS.

Isabel's Teething Biscuits

While my daughter's teeth were still coming in, these delicious and quick-to-throw-together biscuits proved quite helpful during the process. While they do contain sugar, be aware that children under age one shouldn't have honey, so it shouldn't be substituted. Grown-ups, you're going to like them, too!

In a medium bowl, combine the flour, milk powder, wheat germ, baking powder, cinnamon, and salt. Set aside.

In large bowl, combine the sugar and oil. Beat in the egg and orange juice. Gradually add the flour mixture to make a stiff dough. Refrigerate for 1 to 2 hours.

Preheat oven to 375 degrees.

Place greased cookie sheets on a damp towel to keep from sliding. Place dough on cookie sheet and flatten, rolling out to about 1 inch of the edge of the sheet.

Cut into 2 x ¾-inch bars (you won't need to separate the cookies). Bake 15 minutes until light brown.

Remove from oven and recut the cookies on the same lines. Return to the oven. Turn off the oven and let the cookie sheets sit until the oven is cool. These cookies can be frozen up to 1 month, and thawed as needed.

MAKES ABOUT 6 DOZEN COOKIES.

2½ cups all-purpose flour

½ cup instant nonfat dry milk powder

½ cup wheat germ

1½ teaspoons baking powder

½ teaspoon ground cinnamon

½ teaspoon salt

¾ cup sugar

¾ cup vegetable oil

1 large egg, at room temperature

½ cup undiluted frozen orange juice concentrate, thawed

Multicolored Frosted Sugar Cookies

This is one of the best sugar cookie recipes I know of for cut-out cookies. At holidaytime, roll the dough ¼ inch thick and use your favorite themed cookie cutters. Anytime, color a bunch of icing, top with sprinkles, and create a rainbow of beautiful treats.

COOKIE INGREDIENTS:

1 cup (2 sticks) unsalted butter, softened

¾ cup sugar

2 cups all-purpose flour

½ teaspoon baking powder

¼ teaspoon salt

1 teaspoon almond extract

1 to 2 tablespoons milk

Multicolored sprinkles for rolling

FROSTING INGREDIENTS:

¼ cup (½ stick) unsalted butter, very soft

2 to 2½ cups confectioners' sugar

2 tablespoons milk

½ teaspoon vanilla extract

Food coloring

Preheat oven to 400 degrees.

To make the cookies: In a medium bowl, cream the butter and sugar on the medium speed of an electric mixer until fluffy, about 1 to 2 minutes. Reduce speed to low and add in the flour, baking powder, salt, and extract, continuing to beat until well mixed (another 1 to 2 minutes). Add in 1 tablespoon of the milk to moisten the dough. Add a touch more milk if needed to bring the dough together.

Remove the dough from the bowl, roll into a large ball, and start to break off 1-inch pieces. Roll these into balls and place about 2 inches apart on ungreased cookie sheets. Flatten balls to ¼-inch thickness with the bottom of a juice glass. Roll outer edges in sprinkles before baking. Bake 7 to 9 minutes, or until the edges are lightly browned. Cool the cookies on the sheets for 1 minute, then remove to a rack to cool completely.

To make the frosting: Place the butter in a medium bowl. Add 1 cup of sugar and then the milk and vanilla. Beat until smooth and creamy. Gradually add the remaining sugar until the icing is a good spreading consistency (you may not need all the sugar). Separate into 4 small bowls, and add 1 to 2 drops of different food coloring to each (more if desired), and mix thoroughly.

Spread the icing on the cooled cookies with a small knife or small offset spatula.

MAKES ABOUT 2½ DOZEN COOKIES.

Pancakes

Though technically not baking, this is a fun dish to make with slightly older children. You can use special shapes to create your own style of pancakes such as Valentine's Day heart-shaped pancakes.

In a medium bowl, blend the egg, milk, and vegetable oil together with a whisk and set aside. In a separate bowl, blend together the flour, sugar, baking powder, and salt. Then add the flour mixture into the milk mixture and mix well. The batter may be a bit lumpy.

Heat a well-oiled medium skillet on medium-high heat. Ladle a small ladleful of the batter into the pan and cook until the surface of the pancake is covered with small bubbles. Flip the pancakes carefully with a spatula. Cook for an additional 1 to 2 minutes.

Garnish with your favorite topping, such as maple syrup, fruit, whipped cream, confectioners' sugar, etc.

MAKES 6–8 MEDIUM PANCAKES.

★ NOTE: YOU CAN KEEP ALREADY PREPARED PANCAKES WARM ON A BAKING TRAY IN A 200-DEGREE OVEN UNTIL READY TO EAT.

2 large eggs, at room temperature

1 cup milk

2 tablespoons vegetable oil

1 cup all-purpose flour

3 tablespoons sugar

1½ tablespoons baking powder

1 teaspoon salt

Oil for frying

Peanut Butter Chocolate No-Bake Cookies

You can easily cut this recipe in half when you want a smaller yield. This is a sticky recipe, but so simple and fun to make with kids. Just remember to put your pot in the sink and fill with hot water right away.

2 cups sugar

4 tablespoons unsweetened cocoa powder

$\frac{1}{2}$ cup (1 stick) unsalted butter, softened

$\frac{1}{2}$ cup milk

1 cup smooth peanut butter

1 teaspoon vanilla extract

3 cups rolled oats (not quick-cooking oats)

In a medium saucepan, bring the sugar, cocoa powder, butter, and milk to a boil. Let the mixture boil for 1 minute. Turn off the flame and add in the peanut butter, vanilla, and oats, stirring until thoroughly mixed. Drop the mixture by teaspoonfuls onto sheets of wax paper, and leave at room temperature until the cookies are cooled and hardened, about 20 minutes.

MAKES 4 TO 5 DOZEN COOKIES.

Velvet Fudge Pie

Preheat oven to 325 degrees.

To make the crust: In a small bowl combine the butter and the cookie crumbs. Press firmly into a 9-inch glass pie dish. Bake for 10 minutes. Remove from the oven and cool completely.

To make the filling: In a medium bowl, microwave the chips on medium-high for 1 minute, stir, and microwave an additional 30 seconds, if needed. Stir until smooth. Cool to room temperature.

In a large bowl, on the medium speed of an electric mixer, beat the melted chocolate, cream cheese, and vanilla until light in color, about 3 to 4 minutes. In another bowl, whip the heavy cream on high speed to make stiff peaks. Then, gently fold the whipped cream into the chocolate mixture until completely incorporated. Spoon this into the prepared crust and smooth evenly. Chill at least 1 hour, or until completely firm.

SERVES 6 TO 8.

CRUST INGREDIENTS:

$\frac{1}{4}$ cup ($\frac{1}{2}$ stick) (a bit more if needed) unsalted butter, melted

$1\frac{1}{2}$ cups chocolate wafer cookies, crushed

FILLING INGREDIENTS:

2 cups milk chocolate chips, melted

1 (8-ounce) package cream cheese, softened

1 teaspoon vanilla extract

1 cup heavy whipping cream

Metric Equivalencies

Liquid and Dry Measure Equivalencies

Customary	Metric
¼ teaspoon	1.25 milliliters
½ teaspoon	2.5 milliliters
1 teaspoon	5 milliliters
1 tablespoon	15 milliliters
1 fluid ounce	30 milliliters
¼ cup	60 milliliters
⅓ cup	80 milliliters
½ cup	120 milliliters
1 cup	240 milliliters
1 pint (2 cups)	480 milliliters
1 quart (4 cups)	960 milliliters (.96 liter)
1 gallon (4 quarts)	3.84 liters
1 ounce (by weight)	28 grams
¼ pound (4 ounces)	114 grams
1 pound (16 ounces)	454 grams
2.2 pounds	1 kilogram (1000 grams)

Oven-Temperature Equivalencies

Description	°Fahrenheit	°Celcius
Cool	200	90
Very slow	250	120
Slow	300–325	150–160
Moderately slow	325–350	160–180
Moderate	350–375	180–190
Moderately hot	375–400	190–200
Hot	400–450	200–230
Very hot	450–500	230–260

INDEX

marshmallow crunch
brownie bars, 15
meringues, 16
mint chocolate
chocolate chip
cookies, 17
multicolored frosted
sugar cookies, 108
orange coconut raisin
cookies, 18
peanut butter chocolate
no-bake cookies, 110
peanut butter dream
bars, 19
pecan pie bars, 20
cranberry(ies):
cupcakes with maple
cream cheese icing,
53–54
dried, pumpkin bars, 13
tea loaf, 27
cream cheese, 7
black and white
cupcakes, 51
cappuccino cheesecake,
77
cherry-topped
macaroon
cheesecake, 78
chunky peanut butter
frosting, 60
icing, 37
icing, carrot cake with,
36–37
lime cheesecake with
gingersnap crust, 79

low-fat white chocolate
raspberry cheesecake,
80–81
maple icing, 54
peanut butter
cheesecake, 82
pumpkin bourbon
cheesecake, 83
pumpkin icing, 57
velvet fudge pie, 111
cream-filled Splenda-
iferous vanilla
cupcakes, 61–62
creaming butter, 3
creamy vanilla frosting,
45
crisp, pear nectarine, 93
crumb cake, banana
oatmeal, 67
cupcakes, 49–62
black and white, 51
Buttercup golden, 34–35
butter golden, 34–35
chunky monkey, 52
cranberry, with maple
cream cheese icing,
53–54
German chocolate, with
caramel pecan
frosting, 55–56
gingerbread, with
pumpkin cream
cheese icing, 57
Milky Way, 58
our favorite chocolate,
46–47

peanut butter and jelly,
with chunky peanut
butter frosting, 59–60
Splenda-iferous cream-
filled vanilla, 61–62

D

date apricot coconut
pound cake, 66
devilish chocolate layer
cake with brandy
whipped cream icing,
38–39
dried cherry poppy seed
scones, 28
dried cranberry pumpkin
bars, 13
drizzled peanut butter
chocolate chunk
cookies, 14

E

eggs, 4
egg whites:
meringues, 16
separating, 6
whipping, 6
extracts, 4